coleen

SUE EVISON

coleen

THE BIOGRAPHY

JOHN BLAKE

Published by John Blake Publishing Ltd,
3 Bramber Court, 2 Bramber Road,
London W14 9PB, England

www.blake.co.uk

This edition first published in hardback in 2006

ISBN-10 1-84454-335-8

ISBN-13 978-1-84454-335-9

British Library Cataloguing-in-Publication Data:

A catalogue record for this book is available from the British Library.

Design by www.envydesign.co.uk

Printed and bound in Great Britain by William Clowes Ltd, Beccles, Suffolk

1 3 5 7 9 10 8 6 4 2

Photographs courtesy of Rex Features, Empics and Getty Images

Every attempt has been made to contact the relevant copyright-holders, but some were unobtainable. We would be grateful if the appropriate people could contact us.

Papers used by John Blake Publishing are natural, recyclable products made from wood grown in sustainable forests. The manufacturing processes conform to the environmental regulations of the country of origin.

*This book is dedicated to my amazing son Jasper,
mum Irene, to Simon Cowell, an extraordinary man,
all at Syco Music and to fifty people whose names
need no broadcasting – they know who they are.
Thank you.*

acknowledgements

THE author would like to record her grateful thanks to, and appreciation of, all the people who have helped in the writing of this biography.

I am particularly grateful, of course, to Coleen McLoughlin and her fiancé Wayne Rooney, the most down-to-earth celebrity couple I've met in twenty-five years of journalism.

A special thank you to Stuart Robertson at John Blake Publishing for his advice and support. For their encouragement, help, understanding and support I would also like to thank Mark Borkowski, Karon Maskill, Phil Hall, Christina Wright, Stuart Bell, John Blake, Michelle Signore, Nigel Bentley,

Tim Redsell, Sue Bishop, Fran Bowden, Antonella Lazzeri, Marc Giddings, Nigel Gordon-Stewart, Dan Kennedy, Amanda Cable and Roberta Moore.

contents

introduction

AS Wayne Rooney's career moves to ever greater heights there is one person on whom he appears to depend ever more greatly – and that person is his fiancée Coleen McLoughlin. She has remained by his side through thick and thin – and been his shoulder to cry on when tragedy has struck, after he twice broke bones in his foot.

The vice girl scandal, where Rooney was caught on camera visiting a brothel, tore her heart in two. So desperate was he to keep the love of his life, Wayne even offered to go down on bended knee on the pitch in front of thousands of fans to apologise to Coleen, an offer the shy, embarrassed girl declined. Coleen was sneered at for remaining by

Wayne's side. Critics claimed any woman would have walked away – and in ignorance speculated that the only reason that she didn't was because she was a gold digger.

Now they're laughing on the other side of their faces. Coleen has since earned a £5.5 million fortune of her own – and is still as much in love with Rooney as she ever was. If anything, their relationship has matured, each the rock on which the other leans in times of trouble.

One of the biggest sagas in Wayne's life so far has been the breaking of his foot for the second time; the first was in the quarterfinal of the European Championships, against the host nation Portugal, in 2004. Critically, this second break came just six weeks before the first game of the World Cup in Germany, 2006.

From the moment the fourth metatarsal on his right foot broke in a challenge with Chelsea defender Paolo Ferreira, a battle started surrounding his fitness.

The struggle was well-intentioned. Sven-Goran Eriksson, the England coach, wanted the young superstar up and running as soon as possible. He was naturally concerned that he should have his best player available for the assault on the championships.

Medical history was against him, however. Michael Owen took nearly twenty weeks to recover from a similar injury, sustained on 31 December 2005 and Rooney himself had been out for fourteen weeks following the break in his fifth metatarsal in Portugal.

And this was an issue that was taken up by Manchester United manager Sir Alex Ferguson who, from the start, warned that people – medics, the England camp and millions of fans – should be realistic about his recovery. The club boss was looking beyond the finals in Germany towards the new season. He didn't want Rooney brought back prematurely in case it delayed the full recovery of his foot. He was determined that when Manchester United embarked on a renewed attempt at domestic and European glory, a fully fit Rooney would be leading his forward line.

The medical bulletins on the injury started to become optimistic about the chances of England's best player being fit to play in some part of the World Cup – perhaps in the later stages. The daily diagnosis of recovery was the responsibility of Dr Mike Stone, the club physician. He in turn liaised with England doctor Leif Sward to keep him posted on developments.

The Football Association, who control the England team, wanted to hear good news. Not only was Rooney crucial to their plans on the pitch, he was also fundamental to multi-million pound commercial deals as he was rapidly becoming the most famous footballer in the world. If Dr Stone passed on good news, it became magnified in the eyes of those in the international set-up. And when headlines appeared predicting that Rooney was making a remarkable recovery, not everybody was happy.

Sir Alex probably would have preferred a news blackout to allow his star striker to recuperate without the strain of being the focus of such intense speculation. But these days, that's impossible.

And after Rooney appeared with Coleen at a glamorous pre-World Cup party at the home of England captain David Beckham and his wife Victoria, dramatic developments took place. Not for the first time in her life, Coleen found herself in the position of mother-confessor and rock of support to the man she regards above all others. Through no fault of his own Wayne was suddenly plunged into one of the most bitter battles in which a footballer can find himself – that of club versus country.

Following the publication of pictures of Wayne and Coleen at the party – she in a flowing blue dress and he in a sombre dinner suit – the Manchester United doctor, Mike Stone, abruptly left the club. A statement released at the time said that the physician's departure was prompted by 'non footballing and non clinical issues.'

Pictures from the party which showed Wayne wearing what appeared to be a perfectly normal shoe on his damaged right foot were accompanied by reports that the footballer led the dancing. Though there were plenty of images of the night of the couple in the presence of other stars, there were no pictures of him on the dance floor.

But reports like that would have infuriated Sir Alex Ferguson. Not only would Ferguson have questioned what his player was doing out in public, he would also have been irked that it was to attend a party at the home of England captain Beckham.

Sir Alex and David Beckham have not appeared to be close since Beckham left Manchester United for Real Madrid in 2003. It was an acrimonious parting following a number of well-reported disagreements. A few days before the party a report had been issued stating that Rooney was making a 'perfect recovery.' England medic Dr Sward said that he had been in constant touch with Dr Stone and the reports that he had been given were 'very, very positive.' He added that the England camp were very happy to leave the progress of the footballer's recovery to Dr Stone and his colleagues at the club because they were doing a 'tremendous job'.

Wayne regarded Mike Stone as a friend at the club who had been so supportive to him – and who had kept up his spirits – through the early weeks of recovery.

Rooney desperately wanted to be fit for the finals but at the same time he had many times pledged his allegiance to Manchester United and he regarded Ferguson as a father figure. His dilemma was whether his foot was feeling good enough for him to train, and ultimately to play, or whether he should be cautious.

His heart and his youthful exuberance told him he could make it for some part of the finals. But his mind and his check with reality told him he had a glittering career of perhaps fifteen years in front of him and he might have to bite the bullet on this one.

Only Coleen could properly understand his tortuous dilemma. Only a girl who had seen her boyfriend catapulted from the mean streets of Croxteth to superstardom in such a short time could cope with his anxieties. Only a young woman who had accompanied him on that dramatic helter-skelter ride to mega-adulation could comprehend the scale of the forces at work.

The danger is that without an anchor like Coleen at his side, events could so quickly spiral out of control. The best example of this would be the way that Paul Gascoigne's career went after a major injury, although Gazza was out of action for six months, Wayne for six weeks. It was a very serious blow and above all he needed months of rest and recuperation. Injuries can drive players mad with boredom. They are natural athletes and inactivity is alien to them.

Once Gazza was out of bed he became restless. During the course of his recovery he fell over in a loo in a Newcastle nightclub which aggravated the injury. It was a shocking incident brought on by his own frustration at being immobile.

Unlike Rooney, Gascoigne never had a childhood sweetheart who could accompany him on a kaleidoscopic journey through life. His parents were good, well-meaning people but obviously of a different generation. His closest confidante – if you like, his Coleen substitute – was his schoolboy pal and totally loyal friend Jimmy 'Five Bellies'.

But two male pals can't possibly construct the sort of emotional platform of support that mutually holds up Wayne and Coleen. An old-schoolboy pal cannot second-guess Wayne and react in the right way to everything that happens as Coleen can.

Coleen is not fazed by Wayne's fame. She has grown up with it and now shares it. No matter how well a young man knows his mates, they are always going to be in awe of a footballing superstar and that warps the decision-making process. Where Coleen will dispense common sense and present her boyfriend with the facts, Five Bellies would be happy to go out and buy Gazza a thousand lottery tickets, each one filled in individually with different combinations of numbers. These are different types of support.

The saga of the metatarsal break in 2006 is not the first time that Coleen had has to be the stone wall that Wayne leans against when an issue spins out of control.

In 2004, after Wayne had hit the world stage in spectacular fashion at the European Championships in Portugal he left his boyhood club Everton, and went to Manchester United. It was an acrimonious transfer because the process bounced around in speculation and rumour for weeks before Wayne found it necessary to formally ask to go.

People in his home town of Liverpool turned against him. He was labelled a Judas and it was particularly hard for Coleen and their families who faced rancour from disappointed fans. But together they got through it and re-established their lives in the lavish surroundings of the Cheshire stockbroker belt.

Their relationship is a return to old-fashioned values for footballers. Many years ago – in fact at the start of the George Best era – young footballers were encouraged to marry. The nature of the job was that once training was over by lunchtime each day it was better for the player to have a stable family base to return to. Otherwise he might spend all afternoon in the pub or at the racecourse.

George Best broke the mould of this routine by deciding that there was so much on offer in the big wide world that he did not need a reason to go home each day. And he certainly didn't need a wife when he got there. His life became a tragic legacy to that attitude.

Many onlookers will see Coleen as merely Wayne's girlfriend. They will take it for granted that she will always be on his arm. But others who are more informed will realise that she is a tremendously important part of the Rooney phenomenon. She is the only one who has been through the staggering sea change of life that they have experienced – together. Nobody else on earth holds the qualification to be able to understand and help in a million different ways on the phenomenal journey that lies ahead.

This is her story, a tribute to a woman who has stood by her man through thick and thin and knows him best of all.

CHAPTER ONE

from chip shop chic to catwalk queen

IT was the picture which would change Coleen McLoughlin's life – dressed in school uniform, clumpy black heels and a puffa jacket, she stared in startled disbelief as a camera flashed in her face. She was just an ordinary schoolgirl, concentrating on her GCSE exams and hoping that one day she might become a journalist or actress.

Instead, this was the start of an extraordinary journey which would lead her through the pitfalls of fashion faux pas, from chip shop chic and chav street style to becoming a glamorous covergirl, starring on the front of elite fashion bible *Vogue*.

It is a journey which Coleen has managed with style and good grace and, today, she has blossomed into a beautiful woman, even trumping Victoria Beckham at her and David's pre-World Cup bash in May. While the stick-thin Posh wore a lime green dress slashed to the thigh, Coleen arrived in a flattering, off-the-shoulder, powder blue gown, her hair groomed into a bun and glowing with natural health.

She looked a million dollars – and a million miles away from the girl who was pictured by the paparazzi as she made her way to school in 2002.

Explained Coleen: 'I'd been seeing Wayne a good few months then and it was when he was going off to play for England. He'd come round to my house to pick something up and the photographers must have followed him. This man just jumped out the bushes. Then, when I got to school, in the car park there was a man pretending to fix his car, but he had his camera over the top of the bonnet.

'My teacher told me to ring my mum. She was going ballistic, saying, "What if they got me? I've just put the wheelie bin out in my nightie!"'

Inevitably, as the months wore on, the paparazzi became relentless in their quest to capture Coleen on camera. The tabloids labelled her as the Queen of Chav for her downmarket style, mocked her weight and even the myriad shopping trips she made in a bid to satisfy her critics.

2

FROM CHIP SHOP CHIC TO CATWALK QUEEN

It seemed Coleen could do nothing right. From her Burberry check bikini and Juicy Couture tracksuits, to her rabbit fur Muklak boots, she always drew the venom of the *fashionistas* who enjoyed tearing her apart. The snobby scorn didn't just rain down, it poured.

Daily Mail columnist Amanda Platell sniped in 2005: 'No number of designer makeovers can disguise the fact that underneath she is Vicky Pollard with money, just as no amount of crash diets can really change that sweet, tubby little figure. She is flogging her chavdom for all it is worth while she can, as even Col knows she has the shelf life of a pork pie. Let's face it, when it comes to style, Coleen's the kind of young woman whose fashion instincts are stretched to breaking point matching up a bikini. And if she turned up at any model agency minus her £25,000 Tiffany engagement ring and asked for a job, she'd be shown to the tearoom. If Coleen were a stick of Brighton rock, she would have the Burberry check stamped all the way through.'

Comedienne Jenny Eclair, hardly a style icon herself, sneered: 'The notion that Ms McLoughlin is the nation's newly chosen Queen of Chic makes me despair. For starters she's got one of those classic working class bodies – it doesn't matter how gym-toned the girl might be, there is still something about her that looks like she was designed to bring in the washing.

'Here are some facts: you cannot be a style icon and the face of Asda, as Coleen is. That – literally – would be having your frozen chocolate gateau and eating it. Coleen is as exotic as a catering size bag of chips, but possibly slightly duller. She is the Chav Princess.

'Another big mistake Coleen makes is always wearing clothes that are too small. Wearing a size 10 won't make her a size 10. It just makes her look like a person whose clothes are too small.

'She may be a nice girl but I'm as likely to take style tips from Coleen as I am to take elocution lessons from her boyfriend.'

And novelist Helen Frith Powell, expert on French and British style, wrote: 'She epitomises everything that makes British women the laughing stock of Europe in the style stakes. If Coleen lived in France or Italy she would be notorious for being the worst dressed woman in the country.

'Let's not forget that this is a woman who spent the past two years with her belly hanging over a pair of low-slung tracksuit trousers. Coleen looks about as stylish as Sir Alex Ferguson looks in his trackies.'

And the scorching scorn went on and on. It wasn't

until fashion bible *Vogue* took the extraordinary step of using Coleen as a cover girl in 2005 that the *fashionistas* suddenly and grudgingly changed tack.

Coleen, bewildered by the bile she drew, lamented: 'When it comes down to it I haven't set out to be famous but I am beginning to feel like I can't win. Sometimes I wonder if I am being punished for something Wayne has done. In the end, what matters to Wayne is what appears on the back pages, the sports pages – he can go out and be a hero again on the football pitch. I can't. I'm not the person I'm portrayed as – a shopaholic airhead. And there's all this hype but I didn't go out and seek it.'

Coleen effectively became a victim and target merely because she was Wayne's girlfriend. The first and only interview she ever gave with Wayne was with me in 2004 and, even then, it was obvious from her demeanour that she had been stung by the criticism. She was wary, seemed vulnerable and anxious to please. 'I don't understand that "chav" label,' she told me. 'I don't know even what it is supposed to mean. When you see someone in the paper it is so different to real life isn't it?

'When I read that I was the most hated girl in Britain that made me think. So I started thinking about doing more exercise and watching what I eat. If I lose weight from around my face I don't even look like me and I do want to be me. Sometimes when I read what people have said about me it does upset me, I do get upset. It can be hard to take criticism just for being me.'

Coleen believed much of the sniping was down to jealousy which she had already suffered at school when she was first pictured in the newspapers. Bitching about her position and the fact that Wayne was happy to lavish his money on her were part of the reason she had decided to leave school.

She told me: 'You do see jealousy. People will start calling me names when they haven't even met me. Jealousy's a big thing. When people see that you've got money, you're the worst person in the world. And if you've got nothing you're the best person.'

The *Vogue* shoot was a huge boost to her self-esteem. Until then, she had ignorantly been characterised as a grasping female who had abandoned her acting ambitions to hitch herself to a goldmine. She was a mere adjunct to Wayne's world, they said, her dependency cemented by licensed profligacy with his £50,000 a week salary and millions in endorsements.

But now Coleen has her tail up. Although ignorant of fashion, she is unwittingly rewritings its rules. Her typical random attire of a Dolce & Gabbana puffa jacket, tight Juicy Couture jeans and Ugg boots –

once perceived as a ghastly combination – was copied on the street. And the fashion industry has since followed closely behind.

These days, Coleen even has her own fan club. There are teenage girls, grown women, mothers and young daughters who will travel cross-country to Liverpool, from as far away as Milton Keynes, on the off chance that they might spot Coleen in one of her favourite stores. If she happens to be there, in somewhere like the designer boutique Cricket or H&M, they rush up, excited as any boy-band fan could be, and breathlessly ask her to pose for their digital and disposable cameras.

Coleen stands there, arm in arm with absolute strangers, posing for photographs of out-of-town shoppers shopping with Liverpool's most famous shopper of all.

'It's flattering,' Coleen says, 'but I also find it kind of strange. I'm not used to it yet.'

Those who ignorantly dismissed Coleen as a gold-digging, publicity-hungry arriviste hadn't reckoned on her mettle. She refused to bow down and worship at the altar of high fashion, mixing High Street style with designer labels, the way she always had. She was even voted queen of the High Street in a 2006 poll by *Closer* magazine.

'I wear clothes that please *me*, not the paparazzi,'

she says. 'When I had a £3.65-an-hour Saturday job in New Look I would save up for a new pair of shoes or a top. Most girls are like that. And on my 16th birthday I spent all day in town with my mates and we walked around every single shop. That's the way I have always been.

'I've got my own wages coming in now from the work I do but Wayne likes to treat me now and again. He is generous and likes to buy me things. I've always loved fashion but I like to have my own style otherwise I'm not me. I still go to Zara or Top Shop where I can pick up a dress for between £25 and £40.'

Nor was Coleen going to accept the labels she'd been handed down by the tabloids – gold-digger, chav, a workshy girl who was only famous for spending Wayne's money. By her own admission she has always been ambitious to escape the estate in Croxteth where she was brought up and worked hard to improve her lot. The fact that she was the childhood sweetheart of Wayne Rooney was coincidental in changing her life. Coleen has always wanted a career of her own and she doesn't want to be seen as simply Wayne's fiancée, she wants to be a person in her own right.

One of the best things about Coleen is that she has remained grounded. She still has a burning desire to become an actress but she has not abandoned her past. She left school at 17 when she was studying for A-levels because all the fuss surrounding her and Wayne was distracting and her grades suffered. She left because she wanted to concentrate on acting – she was getting offered parts but couldn't accept them because of her school work.

During the day that I spent with Coleen and Wayne she spoke constantly to her childhood friends on her mobile and treated Wayne just like one of them, even grumping at him when he teased her about how easy she was to wind up.

There is nothing disingenuous or contrived about Coleen. She is simply a pleasant girl who has suddenly become famous and wealthy thanks to the fact that her childhood sweetheart – a man she met when he had nothing and wore hand-me-down trainers – became a national hero. That she feels aggrieved at some of the criticism she has received is understandable for that reason alone.

Countless fashion shoots followed on from *Vogue*, including one with the *Mail on Sunday* in January 2006, Coleen recreating the understated style of the refined screen sirens from fifties Hollywood. With her long tousled hair in ringlets, she modelled chic designer creations such as a blue Missoni bustier and full rara skirt. In the magazine's cover shot, a pale blue Stella McCartney top slipped seductively off her shoulder, while in another picture she perched coquette-like on a stool in a yellow Roland Mouret jacket and fifties-style Attica shoes.

The pictures, by acclaimed fashion photographers Michael Labica and Sadrine Dulermo, were the latest stage in Coleen's reinvention – and Dulermo herself paid her a compliment saying, 'There's nothing wrong with Coleen. She is a very sexy girl.' It was praise indeed coming from Dulermo, one of high fashion's most sought after photographers.

There's no doubt Coleen loves to shop – she's said to have a £10,000 monthly allowance from Wayne for clothes alone – but often the shopping bags she is seen sporting contain gifts for others, including Wayne.

Coleen told me: 'I might be seen at Liverpool boutique Cricket a lot but that's because it's my favourite shop and run by a mate of mine. I always find something I like in Cricket, it's the best shop ever. My best buy in 2005 was my Gina boots. I wear them all the time, especially over my jeans. I couldn't get a pair of Stella McCartney thigh high boots that Posh wears. I really wanted those. But I like my Gina boots.'

Like most blokes, Wayne hates shopping and isn't into fashion, flinging on the nearest thing to hand each morning. 'When he goes shopping he gets everything in one go,' said Coleen, 'but if he thinks something looks good on me he will say, "You look dead nice." If he doesn't like it he will say, "It doesn't suit you." He hates shopping, I buy him clothes for birthdays and Christmas and he just slings on whatever he lays his hands on first in the morning.'

Coleen genuinely loves fashion and was saving up for designer togs long before she could afford them. She used to go shopping with her mum and auntie and look at everything, even if she came home with nothing but a hair bobble. According to her mum, Colette, Coleen was a nightmare as a little girl and, if she saw something she liked, would cry and cry until it was bought for her. On one occasion, when she was seven, a black velvet jumper dress with gold sequins caught the young Coleen's eye. Her mum said she didn't want her wearing black but Coleen got her own way eventually.

Coleen has grown to adore the kind of designer labels that put her on a par with the likes of Victoria Beckham. Even so, the girl who can shop 'til she drops because money is no object still has an eye for a bargain. 'What does my head in is when you buy something expensive and you see a knock-off version down the market the next day,' she explains. 'I always pay full price for my stuff, I don't get anything for free.

'I've got an eye for a bargain – I don't like getting ripped off. I think value for money is important. I go shopping with my friends from school – I've still got a close set from my childhood and they often come round to the house for lunch.

'My mates hate going shopping with me because sometimes I can spend hours shopping. If I'm going out to an awards do and I can't find what I am looking for, I get all stressed and go round every shop about twenty times. So, some days, they enjoy coming with me, but on others, they get a bit fed up. We do have some good girlie days, where we'll go out and get something to eat and go shopping.'

Coleen resents the way she has been labelled by the media – as a shopaholic spendthrift – since much of the shopping she does is for other people. Often the stuff in her bags are for her new house, or Wayne, or presents for the family. 'I don't just buy for me,' she explains. 'I enjoy picking out gifts I think my family or friends will like. I do find it annoying. The reason they call me that is because they haven't got anything else on me.'

Nor does Coleen expect her friends to try to live up to her own circumstances. She is happy with small, thoughtful gifts, acutely aware of how short money is amongst her pals, the way it was for her before Wayne shot to stardom. She is as happy with a pair of jim jams from Primark as she would be with a Tiffany necklace.

She says: 'People think it must be tricky for my friends to buy me presents but I like getting little things that people have put a lot of thought into. 'I always tell Wayne to get me little bits for Christmas. I'd rather have lots of little stocking fillers than a big main present. I love pyjamas, so I tell everyone to go to Primark. They do the best ones.

'If I could go shopping right now I'd go to Miss Selfridge for some boots I've seen, some skinny jeans from Top Shop, the black and white stripey jumper from George at Asda and I'd get a tulip skirt – I've got a brown one, so maybe one in black – and some jewellery from Freedom at Topshop and a nice bag.'

Coleen admits she suffers the effects of affluenza – feeling guilty at her new-found wealth after being plucked from a council estate where some people were so poor they kept egg-laying chickens in their garden to supplement their meagre diet.

She feels guilty that she can buy what she wants when other people have nothing, because she knows how that feels. When she was younger her family didn't have much money and she and her mother used to hide the price of clothes from Coleen's dad, Tony. And now she will often take clothes she has grown out of to charity shops or put them in a pile for her friends to choose.

'Sometimes when I'm photographed and there's a story that says I've been on another shopping spree, all I was doing was popping round to my mum's or buying a friend a birthday card,' she explains.

There's no doubt that the pressure of being in the limelight has taken its toll on Coleen. Many of the things she once took for granted – like being able to walk down the street without make-up or dressing up – now lay her wide open to the snipers. She says: 'Actually, I don't enjoy shopping so much now because there's always a camera watching me. It's not nice if you just want to buy a pair of earrings to go with the outfit you're wearing that night.'

Wayne, of course, enjoys surprising Coleen – he bought her an expensive diamond and white gold ring with his first ever pay packet in 2001 after he signed for Everton. He saved up until he could afford something 'dead special', and has since lavished her with expensive watches, bracelets and necklaces.

And as Wayne's supersonic fame engulfed the couple, Coleen was determined to transform into the kind of woman who could hold her own walking down the red carpet – a case of if you can't beat them you might as well join them. She ditched her trademark Juicy Couture tracksuits which earned her the title of Queen of Chav and just two months later in April 2005 she appeared in *Vogue*, the glossiest of glossy fashion magazines.

It was the *Vogue* cover – the most coveted in the world – which confirmed Coleen had the potential to become the sex symbol she is today. Even Princess Diana didn't get an invite to the magazine until she'd swapped her 'Shy Di' hair for a sharper, cutting-edge style coupled with an up-to-the-minute fashion sense.

The ten-hour shoot at a private house in Clapham, south London, saw Coleen try on twenty different designer outfits created in the style and glitz of 1930s film stars. With her slicked back hair, Stella McCartney skirt, Yves St Laurent scarf and Gucci top and earrings, Coleen was transformed into an Ava Gardner-style sex symbol.

And Wayne was 'blown away' by the pictures, telling her, 'They're phenomenal. My God, you look amazing.' In a touching romantic gesture, he even managed to track down and buy a pair of Yves St Laurent designer shoes which Coleen had fallen in love with during the shoot.

Said Coleen: 'I loved the Vogue shoot, it was fun and I adored the pictures. I've still got copies of them, Wayne loves them.'

But social X-ray *fashionistas* were appalled that a working class, curvy girl like Coleen – standing at just 5ft 3in – should be featured on the front of the most cutting-edge fashion magazine in the world.

Vogue editor Alexandra Schulman, however, didn't give a hoot. The highly influential editor spotted Coleen's potential after one of her staff bumped into her while she dined with Wayne at trendy, look-at-me eaterie The Ivy during a Valentine's Day treat.

Alexandra, the high priestess of fashion, defended her decision to launch Coleen as the new Posh, saying: 'We had been thinking about who was intriguing at the moment and Wayne Rooney and Coleen's names came up as a couple who were constantly in the news. One of my staff volunteered that she had seen them the previous weekend having a dinner in the Wolseley restaurant on London's Piccadilly. She had gone over to ask Wayne for his autograph for her son and Coleen had apparently looked sweetly encouraging of this action – he less so. Coleen had impressed her as looking prettier and fresher in the flesh than she did in the paparazzi shots we were all familiar with.

'Added to that everybody was interested to hear what Coleen, previously a mute figure, had to say about her portrayal as public enemy number one. That afternoon the PR team that she shares with Wayne were approached.'

They immediately said that there was no chance of

Wayne being featured but they said they would, however, talk to Coleen. The answer, amazingly, came back 'No'. Coleen, although 'flattered', didn't want to do any publicity either. She had been 'incredibly hurt' by all the press comment about her.

To Alexandra, a fashion star-struck teenager who didn't want to be in *Vogue* didn't really ring true, so she got on the phone to say that although they understood Coleen might be wary, it was not going to be a hatchet job. And where would she ever have better pictures taken?

Both parties went backwards and forwards over the next few days and eventually a deal was struck. Coleen would be photographed for *Vogue* but she wouldn't talk about Wayne. She would, however, be happy to talk about fashion. But no money would change hands: she didn't pay the magazine, and they didn't pay her.

Alexandra continues: 'Now, for many publications, an interview and photo shoot with an unemployed eighteen-year-old with an outrageous shopping habit might not seem to be that riveting, but I felt it had relevancy for us. Girls such as Coleen – and it has to be said there are not many who have the credit card flexibility that she appears to possess – are a relatively recent fashion phenomenon. Twenty years ago they simply didn't exist, but more awareness of fashion, an increasing interest in designer brands and the massive growth of "must have" items have changed the shopping landscape. Fashion nowadays is dependent on sales, not only to the few but to the mass market. The Coleens of this world, with their obsessive interest in the new handbag or hat, or pair of boots, are an essential part of the fashion industry.'

Arriving at the London studio to be photographed, she impressed the magazine's assembled fashion team with her un-made up, pony-tailed look. Naturally, she was carrying a Chloe Paddington bag, that spring's wanna-have item. Her jeans and pink jacket were given the thumbs up, but the team were more dubious about the hair extensions and white-tipped false nails.

'Immediately it became clear that she was a normal eighteen-year-old with normal eighteen-year-old tastes,' says Alexandra. 'Like my stepdaughter and her friends, she preferred her hair to be a bit too flash blonde, she liked pink to an inadvisable degree, lived in jeans and was a bit nervous about wearing anything that seemed to be a bit too grown up.

'Do I think she is a style icon? Absolutely not, but I also feel that "style icon" is one of the most ridiculous and over-used phrases of our time. Do I think she is a role model for young girls? No, but neither do I think that the more conventional, glossy magazine content of upper-class girls and models are necessarily lifestyle role models either. Do I think she is interesting? Yes, because she has become famous entirely through the filter of the paparazzi and the tabloid press and that, in itself, makes her a phenomenon of our time.

'All she has done is hang out with her family and friends and go shopping. Her fame until now has been entirely the creation of others, although it appears that after this *Vogue* shoot, her marketing potential became apparent. She hasn't asked for it and she actually pays good money for her shopping, unlike a lot of people in similar positions who expect to be given outfits for free.

'I recently had lunch with the British managing director of a world famous brand. She had been visiting the company's shops in the north of England where its current range of bags had been a touch slow out of the starting gate. A few days previously, Coleen had been photographed with one of the aforesaid bags, which was credited in the papers as being sold for £3,500, approximately six times more than its real price. Nonetheless, even thinking that the bags were £3,500 a pop, people rang the Manchester store non-stop with orders in the first days after it was seen dangling from

Coleen's arm. Doesn't it make *Footballers' Wives* look a bit low key?'

Endearingly, Coleen refused to conform to the Footballers' Wives style, preferring instead to please herself. And, in true Coleen style, she showed her practical, down to earth roots by reacting without any politically correct pretence when criticized for wearing her rabbit fur boots earlier in the year.

'What's all the fuss about,' she asked, 'rabbits are killed for food. What's the point of wasting the fur?' Her comments incensed animal activists who pointed out that rabbits are bred in tiny cages for their fur and live a miserable existence.

But bless her, Coleen came from a place where the grim realities of life were all too glaring and she wasn't about to pretend otherwise.

The sprawling Croxteth estate she called home is by no means the worst in Liverpool, but neither is it the best. Like many of its kind around Britain, it is a bleak, unprepossessing place, an afterthought plonked on the edge of Liverpool's eastern boundaries and left to lumber towards inevitable decay.

More than half the estate's children qualify for free school dinners and tell-tale signs of wearied neglect point towards the hardships endured behind its doors. Long-derelict buildings, windows blinded by boarding, are masked by grim, corrugated sheets of steel; empty, vandalised shops are imprisoned behind barbed wire and the ominous buzz of police helicopters is often heard overhead.

But there are also signs of hope – new developments mushroom and red-brick terraces with tidy gardens speak of the spirited refusal of many to surrender to the acidic corrosion of pride. The McLoughlin family home was one of them.

Yet Croxteth is a place where the finer sentiments of life need often be put to one side in a bid for mere survival. To a girl like Coleen, using the rabbit's fur seemed pure common sense.

Today, Coleen's fashion role models are Audrey Hepburn and Kate Moss – and she's more likely to be seen wearing the same gear as Kate than slobbing around in tracksuits as she reinvents herself in the most dramatic transformation since Kylie Minogue left Ramsay Street.

She is wise enough to eschew the glaring fashion labels like Versace and Pucci, which many consider chavvy, for more demure labels which flatter her youth.

Says Coleen: 'I steer clear of the flashiest designer labels – they don't suit me, I'm too young. Instead I like elegant labels like Missoni or Matthew Williamson rather than Gucci or Chanel. They're too grown up for me. I recently went out with Wayne to The Ivy, it was dead exciting. Tom Ford and Valentino were there – and I just wore a little coral coloured Temperley dress that I like a lot with a pair of suede boots from Cricket.'

She has also learned the art of accessorising – a girl's best friend when it comes to fashion. Nothing is considered worse in the fashion world than wearing an expensive outfit without the shoes and handbag to match.

'I love accessorising,' says Coleen. 'I've never bought a Prada dress but the Prada sports shoes are great – I've got a few pairs at home. And I love Yves St Laurent shoes – I've got three pairs of their strappy sandals.'

Despite the fact that Coleen has been heavily criticised for wearing garish Juicy Couture tracksuits, she refuses to give them up altogether. 'Juicy Couture tracksuits are comfortable to wear during the day, so I still have them,' she says.

'I love bags. The most expensive thing I've bought with my own money is a £2,000 Fendi bag. I saw Heidi Klum with a pink and black Chanel bag which I loved so I bought one like it while I was in New York and a cherry Louis Vuitton bag in Sloane Street.

'I pay the full price for everything, I get no special favours. I know some people get stuff sent to them but I think that would take a lot of fun out of it – I enjoy searching things out.'

At one point, while Coleen was ridiculed as the Queen of Chav, waiting lists for designer handbags would halve overnight if she was seen carrying one. Today, just a few short months later, the waiting lists grow.

Even so, like many girls of her age, Coleen is self-conscious about her weight and finds the constant jibes about her curvy figure heighten her insecurity.

Says Coleen: 'I try not to be conscious about what is said about me but it is difficult. I'm still getting used to our life. I try to ignore the jibes about my own weight but you can only ignore it to a certain extent. I used to try and ignore it but now I read everything, because my friends text me to tell me if somebody has said something rude about me. Sometimes you just think to yourself, "Well, that's me and you have got to take me for who I am."

'It's hard if I know I have put a bit of weight on my legs and, of course the newspapers notice that too. Everyone sees my pictures. That's hard. But I really try hard not to let it bother me. I was pictured shopping at Kwik Save, helping my mum. People said I was wearing slippers – and I was! But I didn't actually go into the shop wearing them. I was waiting in the car outside and when mum came out I got out to help her load the shopping into the car. But I do admit that I will still nip to the newsagents for a pint of milk in my slippers.

'Sometimes, I'll get Wayne to go, especially if there are loads of paparazzi around. I remember we went to Tesco recently and I wasn't looking that good – like any girl, I still get spots and I was feeling vulnerable – so Wayne got out of the car and did our shopping on his own,' she recalled. 'It did cause a bit of a kerfuffle but he knows that I can get upset by unpleasant pictures and comments, he's dead sensitive where I am concerned about that kind of thing.'

Wayne isn't the only one who can cause a kerfuffle – Coleen caused one of her own after a shopping trip to New York in 2004. Like dozens of bargain-hunting Britons, she walked through airport customs blissfully unaware that her American spending spree could put her over the tax and import duty limit. But unlike others, Coleen's enormous spending power meant she was nearly £15,000 over the limit.

After three hours with customs officers, Coleen finally emerged from Manchester airport after handing over close to £3,000 for failing to pay tax on almost £15,000-worth of designer clothes and platinum jewellery. Like most people, she genuinely had no idea that she was expected to pay duty on the clothes and presents she brought home in her bulging suitcases.

It was a sour end to the trip, organised by Wayne to treat his girl by way of celebrating his debut hat-trick for Manchester United.

These days Coleen has wised up – and especially where her fashion sense is concerned. She has been praised for her professional approach, always turning up on time for photo shoots and complying with requests from stylists and snappers alike. And while her habit of mixing designer gear with High Street stuff has sometimes been a disaster, on the whole she pulls off her own look with an air of confidence these days.

Her fashion sense was given widespread endorsement in March 2006 when she scooped the gong for Best Dressed Female Celebrity at the Ariel High Street Fashion Awards at London's Natural History Museum. She beat off tough competition from Sarah Jessica Parker and Denise Van Outen to win the award, voted for by *GMTV* viewers.

Coleen was amazed by her success. 'It's great people have voted for me' she said. 'I wouldn't have thought this time last year I would be getting this award. I was shocked to be up against Sarah Jessica Parker. I love her. I was addicted to *Sex and the City*.'

She looked gorgeous when she turned up with Wayne to watch a Real Madrid game in Spain in 2005 wearing Rock & Republic jeans, a top from Chloe – and shoes from Top Shop. She looked just as sensational when she was snapped on a night out to see the musical *Grease* with pals wearing a Chloe dress and boots from Miss Selfridge.

And she turned up in a smart white suit with Hermes scarf, Gucci handbag and gold sandals to enjoy herself with friends at the Grand National in 2006. Coleen had booked a £10,000 private box for her pals at Aintree, the home of the Grand National, where they tucked into beer, wine and smoked salmon.

But while she drew plaudits for her simple ensemble, the same could not be said for her friends who drew the venom of critics for their still-chavvy style.

One wrote: 'Coleen looked effortlessly stylish but sadly the same could not be said for her accompanying friends, who looked like they'd covered themselves in glue and dived into a mail order warehouse flood sale. She looked like a filly, they looked like a dead heat in a donkey derby.'

It says much for Coleen that she has remained loyal to her old friends. She has a lifestyle way beyond their orbit and yet she refuses to be parted from the girlfriends who earn as much in a year as she spends in a single shopping trip. These days she has Victoria Beckham's number in her little black book and enjoys shopping sprees with other girlfriends and wives of England soccer stars, dubbed the WAGS. But her dream Saturday night is going out with her mates for a nice meal and on to a bar afterwards.

'I start by going to the hairdressers to get ready for it,' she says. 'After I get home I like to spend some time choosing something nice to wear and then have a long soak in the bath. My friends usually come over, like they always did, so we can get ready together and watch telly or listen to music while we do our make-up. Once ready, we all have a glass of wine while waiting for the taxi to come and pick us up.

'My best Saturday night out was probably the night a huge group of us went to the MEN arena to see Kylie. We all got ready at my house, had a few drinks and then went to the concert where we danced the whole night.

'I'd say my worst Saturday night was the night I spent in Accident and Emergency. I had started feeling really sick in my stomach and everything and eventually I was so dehydrated mum and Wayne took me to the hospital. But because they were so busy we didn't get seen until the early hours of Sunday morning and the waiting room was full of really drunk people. When I did get seen they told me I had gastroenteritis and I was kept in overnight on a drip.'

Coleen is now an assured member of the elite soccer set but she's clearly unfazed by the status. She recognises with acute savvy that it is just money that sets them apart – underneath they are no better than her friends from Croxteth.

She says: 'It's easy to look good when you've got lots of money but it doesn't make you a different person inside. When I first met the rest of the England wives and girlfriends, I was dead nervous, it's like meeting people you've only ever seen on the telly. But I soon realised they were all just like me. Victoria was lovely, dead down-to-earth, not posh or anything like that – and nobody calls her that either. It annoyed me when we got home from Portugal [after the 2004 European Championships] that people were making out that she was stand-offish and hadn't been out with the rest of the girls. It just wasn't true, she was out with us all the time. I got on well with Victoria, we exchanged numbers and I've no doubt we will keep in touch.'

Coleen's trip to Portugal for the European Championships was an eye-opener which helped her recognise that she had no need to feel nervous amongst the other women who were just as much on tenterhooks as she was.

She said: 'It was nice being with the other girls in Portugal, because we were all going through the same thing. We all agreed that we love our men but miss them like crazy when they're not with us. Me, Victoria, Frank Lampard's partner Ellen, Ian Walker's wife Suzie and John Terry's partner Toni all got on really well. I'm still in touch with them. In fact, the boys said us being so close helped bring them closer together.'

Coleen's transformation has been extraordinary – and even lofty newspapers like *The Guardian* have come out to champion her. The paper's Lucy Mangan wrote, 'Her transformation from anorak-clad schoolgirl to Balenciaga-wielding young woman in Juicy Couture jeans has naturally inflamed those sections of the press for whom such change suggests she is guilty of the cardinal sin of getting above yourself.

'Added to which she has had the temerity to remain slightly chubby and Liverpudlian throughout a brace of failings which has led to her becoming the target of various forms of snobbery – first, the ordinary social kind (she was instantly designated a quintessential chav, replete with

Burberry bikini and Croxteth address), and then the newer form of celebrity elitism, which labels her and Rooney the cut-price Posh and Becks. She is also condemned for having broken the unwritten code that women in the public eye must have thighs indistinguishable from those of a baby gazelle.

'Poor Coleen – damned for being ordinary, and then for being not quite ordinary enough.'

And *The Guardian*'s style guru Hadley Freeman added to the applause, saying: 'One of the most pleasing things about Coleen is that instead of mixing mainly with other footballers' girlfriends, she has stuck to her old friends, replete with their thighs and cleavages. And if living well and looking good is the best revenge, no wonder Coleen is looking so happy these days.

'Cynicism being our national currency, it's easy to believe those who paint Coleen in thick, jealous strokes as a common-as-muck bird who knows a good thing when she sees one and is hanging on to it for dear life. It's almost impossible to believe that in Coleen we might, just might, be looking at the last recorded instance of youthful optimism.'

I disagree that it's almost impossible. Coleen is a doggedly determined, kind-hearted girl who has maintained her dignity in a way many other celebrities fail to do. She rarely complains and, touchingly, she likes to help others. Where Coleen is concerned, the best is yet to come.

CHAPTER TWO

sex symbol coleen

COLEEN'S transformation has been little short of a miracle – and doesn't just apply to her wardrobe.

The girl once mocked for being a fat fashion disaster has answered her critics with an astounding make over, from the now glossy extensions on her head, the talon-like false nails on her fingers to her carefully manicured toenails. She has dropped from a rounded size 14 to a svelte size 10 and it's not the kind of body you get pounding the pavements on a retail therapy mission. Coleen has spent hours in the gym, sweating at her local sports centre and swapping fatty takeaways for low-fat chicken, fish, vegetables and salads.

Her health kick started last January 2005, after she

piled on the pounds indulging the couple's taste for junk food – especially late-night pizzas, burgers and Chinese takeaway. It all started after she saw pictures of her bum which led her to be dubbed C-Lo in the media, a reference to A-list star Jennifer Lopez's notoriously big bottom. She was also especially hurt when it was suggested that she must be pregnant. It seemed every flaw she had was magnified through the lens of a camera, making her even more miserable about her imperfections.

But today, Coleen can turn on the style whenever she wants to, looking as groomed and svelte as any model. In part, her fabulously dramatic make over was to please her man. Wayne loves Coleen just the way she is but she wanted to look her best for him. So Wayne helped devise a few simple floor exercises for her bum and tum which she can do at home. She has also been following a sensible eating plan just like Wayne, who is advised by the Manchester United nutritionists.

Coleen hasn't done anything extreme like the Atkins diet but she cut out refined sugar and carbohydrates. She has also cut out all junk food – which she loves. Wayne and Coleen were always particularly partial to a pizza but they have been banned while she gets in shape, although she allows herself the odd treat now and then. Coleen also loves scoffing in the late evening, which is the worst time. So she has changed her eating patterns as well.

But her new look didn't come easy. It has taken nearly a year of rigorous self discipline – and the advice of stylists – to turn Coleen from a walking disaster area to the glowing beauty she has become today.

In 2005, nobody in their right mind would have predicted that Coleen, 20, the teenager from a shabby Liverpool council estate, would become a superbabe, her style copied by millions, including the fashion industry. Her unflattering downmarket dress style, replete with shapeless tracksuits and hair scrunchies, made her look every extra inch a chubby nobody, the kind of anonymous girl you could see down the chippie every day of the week.

But Coleen, like a butterfly bursting from its chrysalis, has undergone a splendid transformation, with the help of experts, which has turned her into a sex symbol. She was even voted one of the world's sexiest woman in an *FHM* poll in 2006 in which two million people voted. She beat the likes of Anna Kournikova, Holly Valance, Joss Stone, Cameron Diaz and Kate Moss to come in at Number 45 – no mean feat for a girl who had been so drenched in scorn for failing to conform to the Footballers' Wives norm. The previous year Coleen didn't even make the top 100.

FHM editor Ross Brown said: 'Whatever people say about Coleen, she's not doing anything wrong as far as British men are concerned. Our 100 Sexiest Women in the World is growing year by year and 2006 saw more votes than ever.'

It has been a massive boost to Coleen, giving her the confidence to tackle her shortcomings and turn herself from an overweight plain Jane into a sleek and glossy prize of gorgeousness.

Her first tentative step on the way to the woman she is today was to join Weight Watchers with her mum Colette. Petite Coleen – she's just 5ft 3in – joined a class at Our Lady Queen of Martyrs parish club, close to her parents' home in Liverpool, in 2005, managing to shed a whopping 10lb and earning a Gold Award at the club for reaching her target weight of 8st 6lb. Every Monday afternoon, Coleen lined up with 40 other women to be weighed at the £4.95 a session class, chatting happily about how she had junked junk food and begun living on salads.

'I realised I was creeping up from a size 10 to a size 12,' said Coleen. 'I was putting weight on my legs, bum and thighs because I was getting too comfortable.

'So, earlier that year, I went to my local Weight Watchers classes with my mum and lost 10lb. It was good because I could still eat the things I liked, as long as I counted the points. When I saw the results, I wanted to try even harder.'

That meant joining a Flexibar class at her local gym – workouts involved moving a bendy 4ft plastic bar in front or to one side in order to improve the body's core strength. In layman's terms it's a good way to get a flat stomach. The Flexibar has been used by physiotherapists in Germany for over twenty years and was originally devised to help eliminate back pain by building muscles in the midriff. Coleen turned to the Flexibar classes – said to be one of the toughest one-hour workouts devised – in the hope of a quick fix, even buying one of the £20 exercise bars to use at home.

But just as Coleen was beginning her journey to a better figure, she suffered a dramatic knockback when revelations that Wayne had visited brothels surfaced in the newspapers. He had even left a note with his signature at one brothel, although he vehemently claimed he'd been set up.

Rooney was caught on camera at the Liverpool brothel where he is said to have bedded a woman old enough to be his mother. To add to the humiliation, headlines claimed the striker was addicted to the thrill of sex with call girls and had visited the brothel on several occasions since his first appearance in 2002.

One of the call girls described in lurid detail how she had first given Rooney a massage with baby oil before performing oral sex and then taking him to bed for a full-on romp.

Despite his denials, CCTV footage appeared to show Wayne in the seedy vice den where he was alleged to have paid £45 a time for sex with the prostitutes. Among them were alleged to be a mother of six who dressed as a cowgirl, a kinky boot wearing 37-year-old brunette called Gina and a 48-year-old grandmother known as the Auld Slapper, who wore a rubber cat suit when they allegedly had sex.

Coleen, devastated when the story emerged, confined Wayne to the spare bedroom and later fled to her parents' home for comfort.

Wayne later admitted: 'Yes, I had been to a brothel, a massage parlour, call it what you like, when I was 16. It was not long after I met Coleen. We weren't engaged or anything and, anyway, I didn't know if it would lead anywhere. I felt so ashamed that I had let her down so much. I've always loved her and always will, so why had I done such a shameful thing?'

Rooney later confessed to his distraught fiancée and admitted that she was devastated. He said: 'When I confessed, that made it even worse because she believed the best of me. She was devastated. It's my biggest single regret in life. I can never sufficiently make it up to Coleen – but I have tried and am trying. I never expected this story to come out from my past and it would not have if I had been just another ordinary lad.'

Furious, torn apart and depressed, Coleen piled on 18lbs while she tried to come to terms with the allegations and Wayne's confession. The couple's relationship hung in the balance for months as tears, rows and recriminations threatened to end their romance.

Coleen returned to her comfort zone of tracksuits and junk food and soon was the subject of snide jibes every time she appeared in public, drawing the venom of critics who snorted with derision at her weight gain and gleefully published damning pictures to prove Coleen had returned to being a frump.

Poor Coleen, despairing and hurt, withdrew further from publicity, refusing to give interviews and, at first, turning down that once-in-a-lifetime opportunity of a photo shoot with *Vogue*.

But Coleen refused to be beaten. A determined, ambitious girl, she had always applied herself to any challenge – and she wasn't about to let the snipers shoot her down again. With the encouragement of Wayne, she hired a personal trainer, Elise Lindsay, who devised an eating and exercise plan which would see Coleen answer her critics with a two fingered salute.

Nor did she dump Wayne. With the counselling of her parents, the couple began to heal the grievous rift, both recognising that their love for each other was more important than an event which had happened before their relationship became serious. Coleen worked hard to forgive Wayne – and to regain her figure with a special eating plan devised by her personal trainer.

She said: 'I'm not a breakfast person but my personal trainer says I need porridge to keep my energy levels up so I have Ready Brek with some raspberries mixed in, and orange juice or water – I drink two litres a day. I don't drink tea or coffee. Lunch is a sandwich or a bowl of soup, depending on what I am doing. I am a crisp eater rather than a chocoholic but I have cut back on snacking. In the evenings, if I am at my mum's, it will be maybe chilli or lasagne. Wayne's favourite is Caesar salad or spaghetti Bolognese. If we go out it is usually for a Chinese – I eat lots of vegetables.'

Her change in diet, combined with Coleen's gruelling gym visits had dramatic results within six weeks and saw her return to a shapely size 10.

Included in her exhaustive exercise regime were kick-boxing classes. She found it a good way of relieving tension particularly by thinking of someone she didn't like or had had an argument with!

Another way Coleen helped herself dispel toxins and get rid of stress was with massage. No one looks their best when they are frazzled after a hard workout so Coleen treats herself to full body massages at Beauty FX in Alderley Edge, Cheshire. So it's no wonder she couldn't wait to show of her new, curvy shape in 2005 frolicking on the white sands of Barbados in tiny bikinis and looking for all the world like a jet-set babe.

She told *Top Santé* magazine: 'I have always been in my healthy weight range but my legs are now toned, my stomach is flatter and my arms less flabby thanks to the gym. I lost 10lb but that was it, the rest was my body changing shape because of the gym – and muscle weighs more than fat anyway, so I don't get on the scales anymore, I just look at the way my body is.'

Just like a majority of women, Coleen has body hang ups – and battles with cellulite. She would like to be a bit taller and have longer legs – especially when she sees girls in skinny jeans wearing flat shoes. Of course, the fact that, unlike these other girls, she gets photographed a lot makes her more self-conscious.

'My body shape has changed so much now,' she

said after her fitness drive. 'My thighs are more toned – they don't wobble when I walk – and my waist is smaller. Okay, I do have a little cellulite but I try not to worry about it. I feel better in myself because I have more positive energy.'

A sensible girl, Coleen is determined to avoid becoming stick thin like so many other celebrities, including Victoria Beckham. The pressure on her is enormous, particularly when she is snapped every day by the paparazzi, but she is aware of the perils and anxious to avoid he pitfalls of fame.

She said: 'I am quite happy the way I am now. I don't want to be really thin. It suits some people but it wouldn't suit me. I will continue to exercise but I won't be on a strict diet – I reckon a little bit of the foods you fancy does you good. I am glad all the exercise is paying off but I still have got a bit of cellulite I am not happy with so I go for regular endemology sessions.'

Endemology is a non-surgical procedure meant to get rid of the lumpy, orange peel skin many women suffer with. It involves dressing up in a skin-tight body stocking and having the areas affected by cellulite worked up and down with a handheld roller containing a powerful vibrating vacuum pump.

Manufacturers claim the process stretches and weakens the fibrous tissues attached to the layers of skin under the surface and so breaks down the fat cells. It is also meant to stimulate localised blood and lymph circulation and increase production of collagen and elastin, which make the skin more flexible and supple.

The treatment causes significant thirst and for 48 hours afterwards users may need to pass water more frequently than usual. To enhance toxin release, it's recommended that users drink at least two litres of water following the treatment.

The 35-minute treatment, which feels forceful but not painful, needs up to fourteen sessions to show results and sets Coleen back £55 a time.

The makers say clearly that it can't perform miracles – you have to diet and exercise as well to see really good results, a regime Coleen bought into.

She says: 'I go to the gym three times a week and work out for just over an hour. And I walk my dog Fizz. It has given Wayne and me another shared interest. We have a cross-trainer machine at home, they are among the best ways to get an all-round cardiovascular workout – and it's brilliant. If I'm going on holiday, I'll spend extra time at the gym or working out at home, mostly because I know I am likely to be photographed and I want to look my best.'

Coleen's transformation from chubby schoolgirl to

svelte style icon involved hard work and discipline. But she's never going to be a gym junkie.

She said: 'I don't want to get too skinny. Madonna looks great because she is so toned but I reckon everything in moderation. When I was on holiday in Dubai [in March 2006] my friend suggested we went for a run round the beach. I said, "Forget that, we're going to stuff our faces instead."

'I am not a big chocolate lover, I am more of a crisp eater and I love my food. But before I went on holiday I knew I would be seen in a bikini so I went to the gym a bit more.

'It is not always easy to stay motivated, though, so I try to take a friend. Wayne's cousin Claire is one of my best mates but she is a nightmare at the gym. She wants to leave after five minutes so I am always trying to persuade her to stay.'

Losing weight has given Coleen back her confidence. She no longer feels the need to hide away in baggy tracksuits and is justly proud of her achievement. She puts her weight loss down to sticking to a 1,200 calorie a day eating plan, cutting down on convenience foods like chips and takeaways in favour of healthier options.

She swapped her morning toast and jam for Ready Brek with soya milk and fresh fruit. She now eats a jacket potato with salad or baked beans

Coleen frolicking on the beaches of Barbados with her fiancé Wayne Rooney in July 2004. The pair are totally besotted with each other – after just a year of being together Wayne got Coleen's name tattooed on his arm (*inset*).

Above: Coleen accompanied Wayne to the press conference at Old Trafford at which he was unveiled as Manchester United's new signing in September 2004.

Below left: Beside the pool in La Manga, Spain, where she joined Wayne and the rest of the England team here during their pre-season training session in May 2003. For both Wayne and Coleen the luxurious surrounds of the training camp were unlike anything they had ever experienced.

Below right: Attending the Manchester derby at Old Trafford, November 2004.

Above left: Coleen has come a long way from her modest Croxteth roots. Here she is pictured lounging beside a swimming pool in Cyprus after taking part in her first *Vogue* photoshoot, April 2005.

Above right: Coleen proudly showing off her sexy toned body in a stunning yellow bikini on the beach in Tenerife, March 2005.

Below: Careful to keep her feet on the ground, Coleen makes sure she still has time for her friends back in Liverpool.

Wayne and Coleen arriving at the FIFPRO World XI Player Awards in London at which Wayne was awarded the Young Player Award, September 2005.

Above and *below right*: Coleen kick starts the celebrations for the 10th anniversary of the Jeans for Genes campaign with a visit to Great Ormond Street Hospital, October 2005.

Below left: Looking sophisticated and chic as she attends the National Television Awards in the Royal Albert Hall, October 2005. Her half a million pound earrings made her shine in a crowd of black dresses.

Coleen looking sleek and stylish alongside Alex Curran, Steven Gerrard's fiancée, at a Childline charity event in late 2005.

Above left: Coleen presented an award at *Closer* magazine's Young Heroes Awards.

Above right: In her dazzling cream and gold Prada dress, Coleen steals the show at the premiere of *The Chronicles of Narnia*.

Below left: Coleen arriving at Old Trafford to support her fiancée, December 2005.

Below right: At the *Daily Mirror*'s Pride of Britain Awards in London, October 2005.

Coleen is known as an avid shopper, but this time she had the perfect excuse – filming a commercial in Knightsbridge, London.

for lunch and has cut back on carbohydrates, with dinner being grilled fish or chicken or vegetables. And, when out on the town with pals, she drinks only white spirits with a diet mixer to cut the calories.

'Wayne is made up,' she says. 'He doesn't say much about it but he is glad that I have got into exercise. We had a gym in the house we rented in Wilmslow and Wayne has given me a few training tips too. When we are at home I tell him what I have been doing at the gym and we chat about it. He is happy that I am happy and, let's face it, he knows a lot more about training than me!'

The couple enjoy dining out, but Coleen sticks to her healthy eating regime, even when they have their favourite Chinese. 'I eat a lot of vegetables and drink water,' she says, 'and Wayne is a healthier eater than me. He always orders a salad for his main course but I couldn't do that, I order meat and potatoes, but that's what he likes.'

Her new health and beauty regime doesn't come cheap – what she spends on looking good is estimated at £3,000 a month. But it is money well spent as far as Coleen is concerned, as she likes looking good. When she was growing up her family were always health conscious. Her dad, Tony, used to be a boxer and always insisted his family take a multivitamin, iron and evening primrose oil. These are habits Coleen still has today.

Coleen's favourite beauty treat is having her hair done at her favourite salon Barbara Daley in Liverpool, which she views as a great pick me up. She says: 'I go to Barbara Daley every six weeks to have the colour done and to Herberts, also in the city centre, to have my extensions tightened every five weeks.'

When Coleen first begun to get interested in the glitzier side of beauty, she was one of the women who looked like they had been Tangoed – as orange as any fake tan. But these days, she eschews the beauty salon for top ups on a sunbed, which are often all that's needed to keep her all-over tan.

One of Coleen's most attractive qualities is her smile and she uses it to cope with the bad times. 'If the going gets tough I reckon laughter is the perfect antidote,' she says. 'When I am feeling rough I smile. And because my teeth are so white and straight people are always asking me where and when I had them done but they are totally natural. I just brush them a million times a day to keep them sparkling,' she told *Top Santé*.

'I try to remember to smile as much as I can because I think a smile can light up your whole face. Even on days when I am feeling rough I do my best to keep a big grin on my face, especially if the paparazzi are lurking. I am not a big fan of lipstick though, I much prefer lip gloss to make my lips look sexy. Wherever I go, I have always got some Chanel lip gloss in my handbag.'

One of her best beauty secrets is plenty of sleep – and Vaseline.

She says: 'I need my sleep, I usually get ready for bed by 10.30 p.m. and I sleep through until about 8.30 a.m.

'I love my Guinot moisturiser and cleanser but I couldn't live without Johnson 3 in 1 wipes. I use them to take my make up off and they leave my skin feeling lovely.

'I like Mac and Nars for their colours but I use a bit of everything. My daily basics are a St Tropez bronzer, up unless I am going out. You can't beat Vaseline for dry lips and skin, I'm never without it.

'My life saver when I've been on a girls' night out is Yves St Laurent concealer Touche Eclat under the eyes – and a good night's sleep.

'The girls at Beauty Fix, the salon I use in Cheshire, are always giving me top tips. They help me out all the time.'

Coleen's efforts in the beauty department have now earned her a legion of fans, including in the media.

Fashion leader Lisa Armstrong, writing in *The Times*, in 2006 said: 'Since being spotted on one of her holidays last June Coleen has been gradually shrinking. Currently, she is perfect – not the etiolated scrawn that smacks of neurotic self-obsession and is the lot of so many female celebrities, but a healthy, normal achievable-looking woman, who far from going mad under the constant media criticism, seems to have used it as a gentle stick to steer herself away from the burgers.

'The new svelte physique is key to her rebirth, confirming her not as a skinny Nicole Richie, Lindsay Lohan or poor old Posh-type victim, but the kind of no-nonsense survivor that Liverpool prides itself on producing by the ferry load.

'So the tide of public opinion is turning in her favour. Yes, she spends her boyfriend's money, but she hardly qualifies as a gold digger – she was with him before he was the Wayne Rooney we know.

'The clothes have improved too, which makes all the expenditure more palatable somehow – Fleet Street's more vociferous editors are nothing if not puritanical. The canary coloured drop-waisted frock horror that she wore in the Canary Islands... has given way to a sleeker, classier YSL-style white dress worn to a Childline charity function, the parade of absurdly priced bikinis is now sprinkled with High Street bargains and she's learnt that she doesn't have to wear her labels all at once. There's even a softening attitude in the press towards her zillions of holidays – and her latest bikini cost £6 from Matalan.'

It is a tribute to Coleen that she has the spend, spend, spend habit of anybody who has lived in frugal, thrifty circumstances and yet knows a bargain when they see one. Nobody can blame her for going shopping potty for the first few months after Wayne gave her his blessing with a £10,000-a-month allowance – hold your hands up if you can honestly say you wouldn't. Put them down again – you're lying!

But she has learned from her experiences, changing from a down-at-heel teenager with no experience of haute couture fashion into a simple style leader. She may not have the impact of a Princess Diana, or the shadowy, drug-fuelled figure of a Kate Moss, but Coleen has inspired millions of ordinary girls with her mishmash of styles and the way she has taken a step up in life, daring to wear the kind of clothes even a supermodel would be proud of.

She didn't get her newfound slim figure by walking the streets of Merseyside, spending her boyfriend's money. It required hard graft, discipline, sometimes even tears, to hone herself into the kind of woman others might look up to in a way that says, 'I could do that.'

It's all very well saying she has so much money at her disposal that she couldn't fail to look lovely. Partly, that is true. But she has also put in the effort herself. Nobody can sit on the rowing machine, run on the treadmill or pound the exercise bike for her – that's an admirable change in lifestyle she can proudly call all her own.

That her efforts are paying off can only be good for Coleen. With a super-fit fiancé at her side, she needs the comfort of looking at least as if she makes an effort to keep trim because she loves him but also because much is expected of a soccer star's wife, not least one of the most famous soccer stars in the world.

Coleen is not stupid and nor is she ignorant. She has always been a good learner – and, today, it is obvious that she has taken lessons from her critics. That she is now being given a break, and even applauded for her efforts, shows that she has the determination, willpower and savvy to want to fit in.

Today, most magazines feature articles inviting readers to capture Coleen's style at a fraction of the cost. It is the beginning of a renaissance for Coleen, the girl who suffered more spat venom than anyone with the exception of Victoria Beckham.

Now that Posh looks like a lollipop head, with a dangerously small size six figure and skeletal frame, there is only one woman who can healthily replace her as a role model.

Coleen has learned her lessons well. Not only has she managed to forgive the man she loves for the embarrassment she suffered when his brothel antics were exposed, but she has steadfastly remained by his side and applied the same dogged determination to her figure, fashion sense and dealings with the media. Coleen has grown into a woman to be reckoned with and, these days, any criticism of the youngster seems churlish in the least. It is a tribute to her sheer hard work that she has grown out of her reputation as a chavvy air-head, all but silencing the critics.

CHAPTER THREE
family values

FAMILY is important to both Wayne and Coleen but she has an extra special reason for staying close to home – her adopted, disabled sister Rosie.

Rosie, aged eight, suffers from Rett syndrome, a degenerative condition that affects one girl in 10,000. Tragically, life expectancy is around 47 years.

Coleen's parents have long fostered children. Her dad Tony, is a former bricklayer, her mother Colette, a former nursery nurse. They married when Colette was eighteen and tried for seven years to have children before conceiving Coleen with the help of fertility treatment. Joe, now seventeen, and Anthony, sixteen, arrived without medical intervention, and then the McLoughlins, devout Catholics, decided to reach out and help others.

Several times, through the church, Colette took sick and disabled children to Disneyland and the healing waters of Lourdes in France. And later, as their own children grew up, they volunteered to become foster carers.

Coleen remembers: 'I was about thirteen when mum and dad sat us down, said what they were going to do, and made sure we were happy about it.'

The first to arrive was Holly, a baby who was being put up for adoption. Says Coleen: 'We had to pick her up from the hospital. It was exciting having a new baby in the house.' Holly was followed by Shelly, another newborn girl and around the same time, through a local authority scheme, the family started providing respite care for sick and disabled children, which became a full-time job.

Then, Rosie arrived. At 20 months old, although crawling and making sounds, she was regressing. The McLoughlins, however, decided they would adopt her. Coleen admits: 'Accepting someone older was a bit harder at first but we loved having her around. There was no way we could have given her back.'

Coleen was fourteen when Rosie first arrived in the family. Tony and Colette already knew Rosie was unwell but had no idea how serious her illness would turn out to be.

Coleen remembered: 'When Rosie arrived she could crawl and even though she couldn't use her hands that much, she would handle toys on her play mat and she could eat. But over a period of time she stopped crawling and lost what use of her hands she had. Then she started having problems swallowing her food. She would cough and choke and bring food back up as she was trying to eat.'

Then, in October 2000, the family discovered the devastating news that Rosie was suffering with Rett syndrome, a neurological developmental disorder. The condition is caused by a gene mutation and, although present at birth, symptoms become evident in the child's second year.

Coleen told the *Daily Mail*: 'There isn't a particular day that stands out in my memory as the moment I realised that my little sister was poorly. It wasn't as if one day Rosie was fine and the next she was very sick. It didn't work that way. It happened bit by bit and it's something we have had to learn to live with and try to understand.'

Explaining the degenerative effect of the illness, Coleen says: 'Rosie can't walk or talk. She can't eat, so she's fed through a tube that goes into her stomach. She has good days and bad days and her health can change from hour to hour. One minute she can be laughing and happy; the next she can be having a fit.'

The family spent their time ferrying Rosie back and forth to Liverpool's Alder Hey hospital and to Claire House Hospice, which offers respite care. Initially, Coleen imagined the hospice would be a grim place where people went to die but, to her delight, she discovered the opposite was true.

'Over the years Claire House has been a blessing to my family,' she says. 'It was one of Rosie's doctors who first suggested to mum and dad that she might like to spend a couple of days there, just to give them some rest.

'At first they couldn't really let go. When you have a child who isn't well, no matter how much you need a break, you find it hard to believe that anybody can look after that child as well as you can. I think mum was scared to allow anybody else to care for Rosie. But parents are allowed to stay in the hospice with their children, and for the first couple of times, that's what my parents did.

'Now Rosie loves it there and the staff and the care are so good. Every month, for a couple of days, she goes into Claire House. I can't imagine it not being part of our lives now.'

Coleen admits the impact of Rosie's illness has

taught her not to take anything for granted and helps both her and Wayne to keep their feet firmly on the ground.

She added: 'Having a disabled child in your family stops you taking certain things for granted, but I must admit that there were things about Claire House that I never gave much thought to. Wayne and I have made donations to the hospice as well as to the units in Alder Hey where Rosie has been treated. But I never really wondered what would happen if people didn't give money to hospices.'

But Coleen would go on a steep learning curve after being approached by the makers of ITV's *Tonight with Trevor McDonald* to take part in a programme about the funding of children's hospices.

Coleen's celebrity, combined with the fact that her sister received respite care at a hospice, made her the perfect presenter on the issue. But it also allowed Coleen to show her more serious side, helping to re-position her in the eyes of the public as a girl of depth and compassion. She said: 'I was quite daunted at first but I decided if there was something I could do that would raise awareness then it would be worthwhile. It turned out that it opened my eyes too.

'The priority at any hospice has to be end-of-life care, but that seems so sad to me because part of the gift that any hospice gives to a sick child is helping them fulfil as much as they can when they might still have a lot of living left to do.

'For example, at Claire House there is a sensory room that Rosie absolutely loves. You can go in there and be surrounded by different light effects and colours and textures. Rosie can't talk to us but you can tell when she is happy – she laughs and giggles and her eyes sparkle. She loves bright colours and being shown new things. When I go shopping and bring back something new she gets so excited. She may be sick but she's still an eight year old girl.'

Coleen was inundated with letters from other families and people who were disabled or dying when it was first revealed that her sister was suffering with Rett syndrome.

'A lot of them said how much it helped to know that there was somebody else in the same boat,' she revealed. 'Some said they had felt embarrassed by their disabled brother or sister but they didn't any more, and that overwhelmed me. It made me feel that people knowing about Rosie was such a positive thing.'

Coleen is the kind of girl who likes to help others. She is compassionate, friendly, warm and giving and that explains entirely her reasons for appearing on the *Tonight with Trevor Macdonald* programme.

Having met Coleen I can testify to her good nature,

her own lack of cynicism and her shyness when placed under the spotlight. She is a bright girl, a deep-thinker and introspective. Her own family's extraordinary generosity has rubbed off on her and she believes it is her duty to be a good role model and to help the less fortunate. She is a modest girl, not one to boast or brag.

She said: 'Having a sick child in the family can be difficult for the children who are well because so much attention and time is devoted to caring for the poorly sibling. But one of the wonderful things about hospices is that they are there for the healthy brothers and sisters too. When Rosie came to us she was just lovely and me and my brothers – Joe and Antony – loved her to bits. She still is just lovely and we still love her with all our hearts.'

Coleen admits that having a disabled sister helps keep her grounded and to recognise that the world doesn't revolve around her. As Rosie's illness has developed it has changed everyone in the McCloughlin household, they have had to adapt. On a basic level, Colette and Tony altered the house so Rosie could have a special bedroom on the ground floor.

Colette takes care of all Rosie's medication and looks after her during the day, while Tony sleeps downstairs to be near her at night when she wakes up or starts choking – she always wakes at four in the morning.

Says Coleen: 'We would all do anything for Rosie and at first mum and dad tried to be there for her 365 days a year. But nobody can do that. Everybody gets tired, everybody needs time to themselves and even though my brothers and I are older now, we need mum and dad too.'

Wayne and Coleen are godparents to Rosie – and she's the only rival for his affections. She's a regular visitor to the couple's house and has a real soft spot for Wayne, as he does for her. He lifts her up and puts her on the bed and lies next to her, singing nursery rhymes or her favourite songs from the cartoons on the telly. 'When we take Rosie out, Wayne won't even let me push the pushchair,' says Coleen. 'He adores Rosie and is dead chuffed to be her godfather.'

And Wayne, who has donated large sums to the hospice, added: 'It's people like Rosie and the kids at the hospice who are heroes, not people on the England pitch. They are the ones who deserve all the praise, they are brave and you just don't realise what they have to face every day. It really is amazing how brave these kids are.

'It makes you realise how lucky you are, especially me. It's an honour to be able to give something back to people who will never have the chance to do what I have done.

'Rosie has stolen my heart. She's very poorly but

always laughing – and Coleen reckons she is always flirting with me. I dote on her. When I buy Coleen an outfit I always buy an identical one for Rosie.

'And she loves our dog Fizz, a chow named after her favourite character in the *Tweenies*. Rosie is always so happy, always smiling, which makes every moment with her special.

'Sometimes, when I look at Rosie, I feel very sad. You get this feeling in your throat... she's such a great kid, like a baby who will never grow up.'

Coleen concedes in her grounded way that having Rosie around hasn't made her a saint – 'I still go out and enjoy myself, I'm just like any other girl my age.' However, she continues, '... perhaps I am more aware of the greater world than I might have been. Even before Rosie came along I knew I wasn't the centre of the universe. We've always been taught what's right and wrong and known you can't be selfish.'

For their part, Tony and Colette have had quite a rough ride with their children. Coleen says: 'When I was four years old they almost lost me to chickenpox – it spread and caused inflammation of the brain. Doctors told my Mum and Dad that I had just eight days to live.' Coleen's memory of the episode is obviously scant but she does recall being in hospital and just crying for her mum because she had gone to the canteen. She also remembers her parents bought her a doll's house when she came home.

Perhaps it's this early dice with death that makes Coleen so thankful for her lot and explains her devotion to Rosie and her feelings for other sick children. Her and Wayne installed a horse carousel, a trampoline and a bouncy castle in the grounds of their new home for Rosie and her pals to play on, after the couple whisked her off to Disneyland for a treat in 2005.

Of course the wealth they have accumulated makes them able to afford such generosity. Wayne told me: 'The nice thing about being famous is that I can treat my family – and Coleen and Rosie and the rest of her family are my family too. I've been able to buy my mum and dad a house and give them and my brothers Graham and John some money. I'm really dead pleased to be able to do that. I'll never forget what my parents did for me. I know they made sacrifices. I want to make them proud.'

The doting son has also treated the his parents to luxury holidays, including that £10,000 trip to Mexico's upmarket resort of Cancun and a £20,000 two-week cruise around the Caribbean on the luxury *Queen Mary 2* liner, a surprise gift to his mum for Mother's Day.

But, as far as his dad Wayne Snr is concerned, the best gift so far is the £29,025 executive box his son has paid for at Everton's home ground. The box boasts central heating, air conditioning and is big enough to seat ten, a welcome luxury for those who would otherwise have to spend up to £33 to freeze in a seat in the Lower Gwladys Street stand.

As a woman with her own wealth nowadays, Coleen likes spoiling her parents from time to time, but to them she hasn't changed and remains the grounded girl she always was. They're fiercely proud of her too, as Colette explains.

She told *More* magazine in 2006 'Coleen's got a great sense of style – like most girls in Liverpool – but although she does love to shop, she's not out every day.

'Coleen's creative so of course she's got ideas for their new house – it is going to be her home after all – but all this nonsense about her demands for £1.5million to decorate it are just not true. That's just silly talk.

'There's a lot more to Coleen than spending sprees and expensive outfits. Her real friends and family know that she is a sweet, caring and bright young lady. Coleen has learned to deal with criticisms about her spending. At first, she found it hard, but she's learned not to take any notice.

'Coleen has to deal with constant speculation about her relationship with Wayne but she is strong, she's got her head screwed on and we're all very proud of her.'

Wayne and Coleen still spend the majority of their free time visiting their parents and, if it had been up to him, he would have celebrated his eighteenth birthday in Croxteth, at the youth centre where he used to play ping pong as a lad. But the venue wasn't big enough to hold the 250 guests on his party list, including high-profile soap and pop stars, so it was moved to an executive box at Aintree racecourse.

Said Wayne: 'Aintree held happy memories for me from when I was a kid. Dad used to take us to watch the horses so it seemed the best place. It was a great day, most of the guests were mine and Coleen's families – there's loads of us, I've got more than 30 cousins living in Croxteth alone, as well as friends from when we were kids.

'It would have been nice to be able to have held the party in Croxteth but the great thing about doing it at Aintree was that I could make it a benefit party for Alder Hey Hospital by inviting loads of celebrities as well.'

The lavish bash, in aid of the Rocking Horse Appeal at Alder Hey, boasted stars from *EastEnders* and *Coronation Street*, Atomic Kitten, as well as team-mates from Everton and England including Francis Jeffers, Alan Stubbs, Michael Owen, Steven Gerrard, Rio Ferdinand and Paul Scholes. David Beckham couldn't make it as he was preparing for a Real Madrid match but sent a video message.

Ford, who have an advertising deal with the soccer ace, laid on seven Galaxy people carriers, each bearing the legend 'Rooney, Street Striker' and decorated with posters of his face, to ferry guests in and out.

Catering staff had spent two days converting the huge betting hall into a banqueting suite for the mega do, unloading more than 100 bottles of vintage champagne for the thirsty guests.

Wayne's cash-conscious mum Jeanette had offered to do the grub herself – she knows her son loves her sausage rolls – but the posh nosh at Aintree has won awards and she relented, happy with the menu. There was still pineapple and cheese on sticks on the buffet table though – Wayne's England mates had joked that they wouldn't turn up unless he asked the catering staff to provide the old-fashioned treat!

The party room was given a New York theme, with a subway train covered in graffiti slogans like 'Roonaldo' and 'Roondog' and 'Wayne 4 Coleen', and an authentic hot dog stand served up the classic American snack.

Above a huge archway were the letters and numbers WR 24.10.85, the star's initials and date of birth, and video screens showing childhood pictures of Wayne played throughout the night. Organisers had also erected a 12ft x 12ft TV screen for guests to bet on horse racing around the world at the do.

Wayne and Coleen had shopped in Cheshire's upmarket Wilmslow for their party outfits; he was in a Versace suit from the town's trendy Norton Barrie store and Coleen wore a little black Dolce & Gabbana dress from the Garbo boutique.

The couple arrived at the do each with three generations of their families – cousins, aunts and uncles, grandparents and parents all waving excitedly from the people carriers as they were whisked into the white-tented venue. And they were met by Michelle Ryan and James Alexandrou from *EastEnders*, Atomic Kitten's Liz McLarnon and Busted's James Bourne, who had challenged Wayne to a dancing contest later in the evening.

Local bands Rough Hill and Broadway Nites got the party swinging and Wayne's granddad Billy jumped up on stage to sing 'Happy Birthday' to his grandson, joined by the thronging crowd to raise the roof to the star, before Wayne and Coleen presented their mums with flowers.

The star went on to make an emotional speech,

thanking his family for their support over the years and officially announcing his engagement to Coleen, making her blush as he wore his heart on his sleeve and paid tribute to his love for her.

Ecstatic Coleen gave her love a diamond and platinum ring and a pair of tickets to see his favourite blue comedian Chubby Brown as gifts – and also a sexy pair of tight-fitting Calvin Klein boxer shorts. Cheeky Wayne stuck them on straight away and then fell around laughing with his footie pals after realising the boxers were the same type as those donned by Arsenal rival Freddie Ljungberg in a raunchy advert!

Later, as the guests mellowed and the party warmed up, Wayne took to the microphone – the star enjoys singing and insisted that a karaoke machine should be provided at the bash.

Said Wayne: 'I sang Oasis' 'Champagne Supernova' – I'm a big fan of theirs – and belted out Robbie Williams' 'Let Me Entertain You' as well. Both me and Coleen love dancing – she used to go to street jazz dance lessons as a kid – but once I get on the floor she can't keep up, she goes and hides and I always wonder why…!'

The evening went off without a hitch but, best of all, it raised more than £100,000 for the Rocking Horse Appeal at the hospital, a cheque Wayne gladly handed over in a presentation ceremony a few weeks later.

Wayne told me: 'The party was great but handing over the cheque was the best bit – it was a brilliant way to celebrate my eighteenth, I was really made up. To be able to do something like that is a privilege and I don't forget that.'

Just five months later, in March, Wayne helped organise Coleen's own eighteenth but, this time, the cocktail of a £10,000 free bar and more than 300 guests proved a tactical error.

Coleen wanted her party kept simple and her mum Colette and dad Tony, who still lived on the Croxteth estate, insisted on paying for the bash themselves, as any proud parents would. The couple hired the £400-a-night Botanic function room at the Devonshire House, a sedate three-star hotel on the edge of the Merseyside estate and conveniently close for most of their relatives.

The evening began well as the guests arrived in high spirits, a large majority of them members of the Rooney and McLoughlin clans, sprinkled with Wayne's pals from Everton and the couple's childhood friends.

The room had been decorated with pictures of Coleen, showing her growing from childhood through schoolgirl to the cute beauty she has become today, and swathed in the Everton colours of royal blue and white. It looked stunning, a thoughtful, fitting tribute to Coleen and the man she had chosen to be her future husband. Both her parents adore Wayne and he has already become like a son-in-law in their affections, spending much of his youth at their home watching telly with Coleen and her brothers on their sofa.

The couple have known Wayne's mum and dad for many years. Tony, once a keen amateur boxer, had helped run the gym where Wayne's dad had also boxed and where his children would follow in his footsteps, and both sets of parents had grown up on the Croxteth estate.

The bash was a gathering of the clans, a celebration of Coleen's birthday but also the fact that the families were now united by the love of Wayne and the girl he had chosen as his future wife.

It was an evening at which emotions ran high, where two sets of proud parents recognised their children achieving adulthood and where wistful reminiscences caused the occasional sentimental tear. Almost inevitably, as at almost any family do where people are flung together in close proximity with a hefty dose of booze thrown in, the night would end with a drunken scrap.

But not before delighted Coleen cut the enormous

birthday cake her parents had made, complete with a marzipan figure of herself on top, and a local DJ whipped up the tempo, inviting the party-goers to take their turn on the karaoke machine.

One of the first up was Wayne, singing a version of Travis' 'Why Does It Always Rain On Me' before launching into a romantic Westlife number, his arm round Coleen as he looked into her eyes, making her giggle, before he gave her a beautifully wrapped gift – a £4,000 diamond bracelet.

The couple handed out gifts to their families and Coleen made a speech, thanking her relatives for coming, before the guests took to the dance floor again, Wayne grabbing his fiancée for a smooch as the lights dimmed.

The star had put £10,000 behind the bar, determined Coleen's party should be remembered as every bit a fabulous an occasion as his own had been at Aintree. As the night wore on, the men took to the karaoke, belting out Everton songs from the terraces, swaying in merry unison and trying, but failing, to get embarrassed Wayne to join in – he might be a star player but the night belonged to Coleen and he wanted it to stay that way.

By 2 a.m., seven hours after the party had started, the booze had run out and the guests were supposed to leave. But, as often happens, some didn't want the fantastic evening to end and the good cheer evaporated when one of the guests jumped on a table, demanding bar staff provide more booze.

Chaos ensued, leading to a rumpus as relatives waded in valiantly, trying but failing to cool the soaring, alcohol-fuelled temperature. Horrified Wayne and Coleen left in tears, the fuming soccer ace distraught that his fiancée's bash had been ruined by the spat and even punching a wall in frustration.

Says Wayne: 'I was gutted that Coleen's party was ruined by a few people who couldn't behave. It was just a family party and sometimes things do get heated when people have had too much too drink but I was still furious. There were over 300 guests, friends and family at the party and only a dozen of them could not behave.

'Coleen was heartbroken and I don't mind admitting I cried too. I wanted the evening to be special for Coleen – we did have a good time but I was angry that it was spoiled at the end. It's fair to say a few cross words were exchanged later on, everyone was hurt and emotional.'

News of the spat led to claims of a rift between Wayne and his mum and dad and between the two sets of parents.

'That's all rubbish,' insisted Wayne. 'It was just one of those situations you wish had never happened, nothing more. It blew over almost as soon as it began. My mum and dad are the people who help me keep my feet on the ground. If I started giving it big time, my dad would just give me a slap!

'He certainly would let me know about it. I still ask my dad what he thinks because I know he will be straight with me and tell me if I played well or crap. To be honest, I more or less know myself how I've played but I still like to hear his opinion.

'It's important to me and Coleen to be close to our families. What's happened to me, all the fame and that, makes no difference. We need the support of our families.'

Wayne's parents had wanted to remain on the Croxteth estate where they had first met, his mum especially wanting to stay close to her own friends but, as Wayne's fame escalated, their wish was impossible. Fans and reporters constantly knocked at their door. Thugs slashed the tyres of the family's cars and their home was attacked with paintball pellets.

So Wayne insisted on buying them the house in nearby West Derby, first offering to send them on holiday while their new home was decorated. True to her down-to-earth form, Jeanette asked for a £250 three-day break to Butlin's holiday camp in Minehead, Somerset, for the family, a treat which had to be cancelled at the last minute when details were leaked to the press.

The couple's new home, boasting en-suite bathrooms, balconied bedrooms, bay windows and a double garage is in Sandfield Park, a ten-minute drive from Croxteth and surrounded by top of the range security. But it was a wrench for the couple to leave behind the home where their happy memories remained – so Wayne gave his dad the £18, 630 to buy it as an investment property and keep it in the family, taking advantage of a 60 per cent discount under the council's right-to-buy scheme.

And it was put to good use. It became a new home for Wayne's unemployed cousin Lisa, a single mum who was struggling to bring up her two children in a grim, mouse-infested house on the Croxteth estate.

She says: 'What Wayne has done for me is typical of him... he's always been really kind and he's close to all the family. Our Wayne isn't the kind to have his head turned by fancy things or people. He's always been one of the family – and so has Coleen. They both love their families more than anything.'

Wayne's aunts, uncles and cousins couldn't agree more. Aunt Janet Gildea, his mum's sister, says: 'No matter how famous Wayne becomes he still comes round for his tea. He is a down to earth lad and has a sensible head on his shoulders.'

And her daughter, Wayne's cousin Toni, says: 'We were great mates as kids and had our little secrets and that's the way it still is. Wayne hasn't changed and nor has Coleen.'

However, the couple learned their lesson about mixing their families and copious amounts of booze by the time it came to celebrating Coleen's 20th birthday, arranging two parties in one.

The night started with Coleen and her girlfriends enjoying copious quantities of Louis Roederer Cristal champagne at £190 a bottle and Dom Perignon Rose at £275 a time. By the end of the evening, the bar bill was £12,000 and still rising. But thankfully there was no repeat performance of the Wild West antics which had so spoiled her 18th.

The McLoughlins and the Rooneys foregathered at separate venues in Liverpool, where the footballer and his wife-to-be gave them a stern warning not to ruin the night.

They then travelled to the restaurant in matching executive minibuses.

Coleen handed out Smirnoff Ice alcopops to her family and girlfriends on the Croxteth bus, while Wayne led a singalong on the other vehicle from the Everton area and distributed bottles of Budweiser. The families' only communication during the hour-long journey happened when the two drivers flashed their lights and hooted at one another on the M62.

Arriving at the Moulin Rouge themed Lounge Ten restaurant, the McLoughlins filed in first, followed shortly by the Rooneys. Inside, the rival families – the Rooneys remain Everton fans despite Wayne's job with Manchester United while the McLoughlins are staunch Liverpool supporters – were kept on separate floors of the three-storey venue. They drank their separate ways until it was time for each and all involved to sit down to dinner in a third room.

The menu included jerk chicken supreme, sweet potatoes, tournedos of salmon and a fried plantain medley. Following that came a wide selection of desserts liberally lubricated with fine red and white wine.

At midnight, Coleen was presented with a chocolate cake – and roared with laughter when she saw the two-tier confection decorated with icing bags carrying brand labels of her favourite stores.

Entertainment came from two jazz musicians playing a medley of classics before a large karaoke machine was wheeled into the centre of the dance floor. Coleen took to the karaoke machine in The Boudoir room where she belted out her favourite Atomic Kitten tune 'Whole Again' while Rooneys and McLoughlins sang along in harmony.

Large star-shaped balloons, carrying the birthday girl's name, filled all three party rooms. Ever the joker, 20-year-old Rooney spent much of the latter part of the evening bursting the balloons and impersonating various guests and friends – but only on his side of the family.

Coleen, dressed in a floaty cream miniskirt, black strappy top and wearing a £10,000 jewel-encrusted crucifix necklace given to her as a gift by Wayne, was one of the first to have her palm read by a clairvoyant hired for the do.

Whatever the future holds for Coleen, she's the girl who has got it all – and still has marriage and children to look forward to.

CHAPTER FOUR

love, love me roo

UNLIKE most footballers, Rooney's romance with fiancée Coleen began way back when he was a fourteen year old schoolboy, and those solid foundations are what have sustained the couple's relationship through stormy times.

Not only did Coleen suffer the humiliation of discovering her man had visited brothels, but later faced another storm when pretty brunette Emily Fountain claimed he took her to a private room in a nightclub then kissed her and fondled her bottom.

The IT salesgirl, 21, allegedly told friends that she enjoyed kissing Rooney at the trendy Odyssey bar in Altrincham, Cheshire while he and team-mates Wes Brown and Rio Ferdinand celebrated their 1–0 win over Chelsea on 6 November 2005. Both later admitted to a kiss and cuddle – and again Wayne confessed all to Coleen.

This latest incident drove the incensed lass to throw her £25,000 engagement ring into a squirrel sanctuary near their former Formby home, causing treasure hunters to gather in the hope of finding the booty. Coleen warned Wayne that he was in the 'last chance saloon' but accepted that the nightclub snog was just a bit of drunken 'silliness'.

And the trials and tribulations of fame, the dirty linen being washed in public and the heartbreaking allegations have served only to forge a deeper love between the couple.

Says Coleen: 'He is the person I love and who I want to stay with for the rest of my life. Friends and family had warned me against dating him. They also tried to persuade me that we were too young to set up home but I have no regrets because I will stand by him no matter what. I had no hesitation when Wayne proposed to me – we've been engaged two years now. People think we are too young but I don't believe that. If you are in love and want to spend your life with someone it doesn't matter what age you are. My mum Colette was married at eighteen and recently celebrated her 25th wedding anniversary.'

The couple's three-year romance has survived despite the brothel incidents and the subsequent kiss-and cuddle with Emily. And says Coleen: 'There are some evil and jealous people out there who clearly want to spoil things between me and Wayne but there are more important things to think about and they should give it a rest.

'Nothing will come between us. We'd barely been together a year when he got my name tattooed on his arm. Now we're still happily together after three years and I think it is a lovely, lasting gesture. I'm so in love.

'Wayne even calls me before every match and from the moment I wake up in the morning I think about him all day.

'Wayne is happy that I am happy and vice versa. We're engaged so we're going to get married. We love each other and that means we will be with each other as long as we are alive. He tells me he loves me all the time. When I am with him, I am really relaxed. He is really caring. You wouldn't think so on the pitch, but there is a soft side to him.

'I trust him completely. He knows his own mind. He knows when people are trying to use him. But he doesn't let people know it.'

Coleen may be just twenty years old but, as the first journalist to interview the couple, I can confirm she is wise beyond her years. The couple's intimacy was unflinchingly demonstrated throughout our interview. Wayne was immensely protective of Coleen and clearly hopelessly in love with her. He was careful to drape a reassuring arm around her when they were in company and was unselfconscious about the unabashed affection he felt for her, tenderly stroking her leg or the side of her face without hesitation or embarrassment.

They looked to each other constantly for approval, she shyly under her lashes while his knowing blue eyes met hers with a steady, piercing gaze. It was clear there was a deep bond between them, born of an enduring friendship and the kind of honest intimacy which can only grow over time. Wayne was unashamedly besotted and didn't care who knew it, his gaze only ever momentarily straying from the 5ft 3in girl snuggled by his side.

'We're a team, that's the way it is,' he told me and it's clear that has never changed. He worries for her, because he recognises with an acute and unexpected awareness that she is coping with the pressures of fame, because of him and for him.

Wayne told *The Sun*: 'She's the most special person in my life. Coleen's not just beautiful on the outside, she's beautiful on the inside as well. She's gorgeous looking but she's also got a great personality, she's a dead special person and I can't think of anyone who is a patch on my Coleen.

'From the moment I first kissed her I always knew she was the girl for me and that feeling stayed strong and never changed. I enjoy every moment with her – and she's about the only person I know who can get me to change my mind. I can be quite stubborn.

'I want Coleen to be happy. That makes me happy. It worries me that she might feel lonely when I'm out training or whatever so I'm always encouraging her to go out shopping, to see her mates and do her own things. I want her to enjoy life. What I'm doing, it's for us, not just me.'

It was Wayne who romanced Coleen, not vice versa – and she made him work at it the way she still does. If anything, he is more in love with her and more in need of her genuine frankness and friendship than ever before.

He says: 'She's my best friend, my lover, my everything. I'd do anything for her and I know she would do the same for me. There is nobody closer to me than Coleen. I'm not the kind of person who trusts easily, I don't jump in feet first when I meet people. Coleen is the only one I trust 100 per cent.'

Despite his fame and the glossy gold-diggers who throw themselves at him, Wayne jealously guards Coleen... and gets jealous if other men flirt with her.

He was livid on one occasion when he misread a text message on Coleen's mobile phone and thought she had a secret admirer.

Coleen told *Marie Claire*: 'He went, "Who's this Sam?" thinking it was some lad.

'I'm going, "What are you going on about, who's Sam?" I grabbed back my phone and he'd mistakenly been reading the time one of my mates had sent the message – 5AM.'

Wayne has a reputation as a shy boy, a youngster who needs to let his magic boots do the talking and with an aggressive edge born of his upbringing on the streets. But it couldn't be further from the truth. Meet him in the flesh and it's a revelation – warm, funny and extrovert, Wayne could talk the hind leg off a donkey… and does!

He enjoys nothing more than sending himself up and is refreshingly honest when it comes to wearing his heart on his sleeve. There's no artifice to Rooney – what you see is what you get. And what you get is a charming, streetwise lad with a sharp wit and shrewd eyes.

He may be a powerhouse on the pitch, a presence so electrifying he seems to fill the TV screen, tackling his foes with the type of bulldozing ruggedness which makes him seem like a Rottweiler.

But, surprisingly, he's just 5ft 10in and, despite his

broad shoulders, is no man mountain. He's about as threatening as a pussycat – and just as playful, sending himself up to make Coleen laugh.

Says Wayne: 'People think I am this shy boy but when you get to know me I can actually be quite loud. I do take a while to come out of my shell, I'm quite cautious but I'm a lad whose Michael Jackson impression can clear the dance floor – and I can sing like Will Young. I've always loved singing. I'm always saying to Coleen if I hadn't been a footballer I would have got into the last ten of the *X Factor*.

'Coleen can laugh – and she does, especially when I sing to her in the morning, usually something by Usher... it's the music I use to psyche myself up before a game. Or I'll belt out a bit of Robbie Williams' 'Let Me Entertain You' or something by Will Young.

'When we were younger I had a karaoke machine in my room and I'd stand there singing slushy Westlife numbers or the Stereophonics. I also loved 50 Cent, Eminem – and Lionel Richie. Sometimes I didn't quite get the high notes but I still like to practice on Coleen.

'I also enjoy a good dance. In fact, I bought a Michael Jackson DVD so I could practice my moves at home before we went to Euro 2004 – and my moonwalk was as brilliant as ever!

'I enjoy making Coleen laugh – and she enjoys

making me laugh. But it can be difficult when we go out because people constantly ask me for autographs, which I don't mind, but we also get girls coming up and targeting me because I'm a footballer. Coleen doesn't say anything because, if she does, she knows she will look like the bad person in the end.

'Fame does mean we can't lead a normal life – we have people sitting outside our house in cars – and sometimes it does get to us but neither of us would complain because that's the price you pay, it comes with the job.

'The thing is our circumstances have changed, but we haven't. I am still Wayne who sat on the wall eating a bag of chips to Coleen and she is still the girl I stole a kiss from behind the church. We know each other in a rock solid way and people can say what they like about our relationship, but we're the only two who know the truth. We're very happy. We have a lot of fun together.

'I can't speak highly enough about Coleen, she's just amazing, my soulmate. She's a special lady. She's dead clever too – much cleverer than me but, then, I sing better in the bath!'

While Wayne heaped praise on Coleen, she giggled and gave him sideways glances, raising her eyes to the ceiling, especially over his crooner claims.

'He's just a dead bighead,' she said, and dissolved

into giggles as he blustered in mock disagreement, telling how Wayne once donned a peroxide-blonde wig Coleen had used when she played Sandy in a school production of *Grease* to take her out.

He insisted they go into town – but Coleen knew him too well to let him get away with a wind up. While he stood at the bar, sipping a Diet Coke and looking a right lemon, she popped off to the ladies – then hid behind a post, making it look like he was simply an oddball all on his own.

And Coleen is just as good a wind up merchant herself.

In the summer of 2006, she took part in a TV programme called *Rio Ferdinand's World Cup Wind Up* – and left Wayne blushing. It was a prank show in the style of Noel Edmonds' Gotcha's and all the victims were members of the England football team. The scenario was that Wayne and Coleen had been invited to a dogs home, but Coleen was in on the joke.

'Firstly they spelt our name wrong on the plaque – Ronnie, instead of Rooney' explains Coleen. 'Then they took us to an operating theatre to see a dog. A vet asked us to watch him – but while he was away the heart monitor stopped and Wayne panicked. The vet then rushed back and told Wayne he would have to break the news to the dog's owner – a young boy fan. Wayne was in shock, but dissolved into giggles when Rio emerged to tell him it was a set up. His face was a picture!'

Watching the couple together was touching. They are each the prop on which the other leans, like two peas from a pod, sharing a closeness and understanding that comes from a shared background and shared values. He watched her like a hawk, discreetly but always with the desire to make sure she was content and to let her know she was the focus of his admiring attention.

Suggestions that theirs is nothing more than a teenage infatuation which will run its course or, worse, run off course due to his celebrity status have proved premature and unfounded. If anything, Wayne seemed the keener of the two and didn't mind who knew it.

Wayne's reliance on Coleen should not be underestimated. He credits her as his soulmate, the person who knows him best and who helps him keep his feet on the ground.

He said: 'Coleen won't let me start thinking I'm something I'm not, she keeps me where I belong, down to earth. People pay you all these compliments and it's an honour but you could start to believe it if you're not careful. Coleen never lets that happen. Our relationship has come a long, long way and there's nothing we don't share.'

It's not surprising Wayne is so besotted. Coleen is a likeable girl, all soft curves and glowing skin, untainted by cynicism and with a vulnerable air which would make anyone want to give her a hug. Her smile lights up her face, showing off beautiful, gleaming white teeth and the kind of graceful cheekbones a supermodel would envy.

She was thrilled by the rows of dresses filling the rails at our photo shoot in the posh Knowsley Hall, just seven miles from the terraced house in Croxteth where she lived with her parents. She confided that she'd always loved designer clothes, getting her mum to buy her outfits from her favourite store, Cricket, in Liverpool but was just as happy to don a Top Shop dress, always looking to Wayne for a nod of approval.

Coleen loves to shop – but she also loved being made up during our shoot – 'it's such a treat, I love the feeling of being spoiled,' she said, and couldn't have been more co-operative or uncomplaining.

It was a long day, and by the end of it we were all tired, but, despite the fact that the couple had another engagement and Wayne's foot was still in plaster after his 2004 injury, they remained until the job was finished – a courtesy many would not have extended.

Today, Coleen remains just as unpretentious and likeable but she's nobody's fool.

Behind her clear eyes there's the tick-tock of a bright, clever mind – like Wayne, she has a stash of life wisdom invested by sound parenting.

Says Coleen: 'I have been with Wayne from the start of all this so I'm getting used to it. We don't discuss money, it is not important to us. Wayne has bought me a few presents and sometimes he treats me, but he doesn't spend loads on me like people probably think. We're still just ordinary people. We have a glass of wine and watch TV, usually the soaps and then go to bed where Wayne will watch a DVD and I fall asleep.

'I think 10 p.m. is late, but then I have to get Wayne up for training with a cuppa because he hates getting out of bed.

'We call Monday night Mad Monday because we watch *Emmerdale*, *Coronation Street*, *EastEnders* and then Corrie again – that's our night in, watching the soaps. Wayne never used to watch them but I think I got him into it.

'We've got Sky+ now which is great. So sometimes we'll tape all the soaps and watch them after the football match. He watches every match, whether it be the Italian league, Spanish league… if they're not on, he'll find a Chinese match or something. Sometimes he goes too far, so I just moan and stuff. But if there's an important match, the Premiership, it's his job, and so he goes down to my mum and dad's and watches it with my brothers,' she told *Marie Claire* magazine.

Wayne and Coleen enjoy their cosy nights in and like other couples, particularly those who are such close friends as well, they find it hard spending time apart. With Wayne's football commitments for Manchester United and England he can be away a lot is Coleen thinks it is healthy to have space in a relationship and she makes sure she is never on her own.

And absence makes the heart grow fonder. 'When Wayne has been away, it's exciting and we can't wait to see each other,' explains Coleen. She is pragmatic about the time she spends apart from Wayne – and reckons it makes it sexier when they get together. 'If we were together constantly it wouldn't be so special. We love doing simple things, like snuggling up on the sofa and watching the *X Factor*. It's Wayne's favourite, we both think it's dead good. I used to watch *Footballers' Wives* in the early series but not now. Now I just turn it off. It's far, far removed from reality, believe me.'

Of course, when Wayne is away he can always console himself with the thought that his shapely fiancée is warming the bed for him.

'Wayne loves my curves. I've always had a shapely

waist. I'm a curvy woman and that's just how I like it. I'll certainly never be one of those celebrities who becomes really skinny. I just love my curvy bum and hips too much – and so does Wayne! But I only ever wear a G-string if I'm wearing something tight. Otherwise I prefer proper pants as they're much more flattering.

'Wayne adores how shapely I am and is forever grabbing me round the waist. But he hates my Juicy Couture tracksuits. He says my bum looks too big in them. But they're comfy and I don't care what I look like in them. I don't worry too much what Wayne thinks. As long as I'm happy with my body, he's happy with it too.

'To show off my curves I wear lots of 1950s-style clothes, like pencil skirts, heels and big belts pulled in at the waist. It's such a good look for shapely girls like me who are proud to show off their curves. I think my best feature is my shoulders. I love showing them off in strapless tops and dresses. I think they're sexy – much sexier than flashing a bit of cleavage.'

However, Coleen, voted one of the world's top 100 sexiest women by *FHM* magazine readers, intends to stay under wraps as far as revealing magazine shoots are concerned.

'I've been asked to do lads' mag shoots but I don't think so,' she says. 'I'm not really a glamour type of girl – I'm more of a girls' girl. I've been asked to do that stuff before but I have always said no. I'd never say never, but not at the moment.

'The only person whose judgement I care about is Wayne. He never gives me advice on clothes. He hates clothes shopping – he just bungs on the nearest thing to hand, he's not into fashion. But he is always appreciative of the way I look. If he does pick something I tend to go for the opposite! If I like something I wear it but I am quite conservative in the way I dress. Wayne and my dad would kill me if I wore anything too revealing.'

People have often discussed with Coleen what a big leap their change of lifestyle must have been but she doesn't see it that way. She admits that there is a difference in the attention she gets now but stresses that she is still the same person underneath.

Said Coleen: 'I don't think I have ever been in a position to take my feet off the ground because of my strong family background and having my friends around me. It's impossible for me not to be me anymore. It just wouldn't happen.

'I get criticised for the things I wear or the way I look but I'm not going to dress up for the paparazzi every day. People shouldn't be judged on what they wear. Some days I will be lush because I have put on a nice top and jeans to go and see my mum and then the next day I can be dressed in an old tracksuit looking terrible, usually all sweaty from the gym. You can't worry about it.'

One part of life that has undoubtedly changed for them since fame and wealth took hold is the holidays they now enjoy and the material possessions. 'I'd say the biggest change in my life is that I have done so many more things and travelled a lot which has been amazing,' says Coleen. 'When I was young we would go on family holidays but not to the extent of being able to have a weekend in Madrid or fantastic holidays in places like Dubai, Mexico and Barbados. I think that's one of the highlights now.'

It may well be a highlight of Coleen's life that she can enjoy lavishly expensive holidays but even she isn't immune to the possibility of tragedy striking. While the couple were on their first romantic holiday in Mexico in the summer of 2003, Coleen nearly drowned when strong currents dragged her out to sea. The petrified lass frantically waved at Wayne as he sat on the beach, unaware of her terror.

He said in his autobiography *My Story So Far*: 'I thought she was waving at me, not waving for help. She had gone for a swim and went out quite far and found herself in rough water. When she was about

50 yards out she started getting into difficulties and began signalling for help. I suddenly realised she wasn't waving, but drowning.'

Superfit Wayne raced into the water, swimming as fast as he could go to reach her. The waves and undercurrent had been so strong that it had even pulled off her bikini bottoms.

He managed to drag choking Coleen back to shore safely. He said: 'She'd had a terrible fright but I'd saved her life. All she could say was, "My hero".'

The couple's lifestyle may have changed dramatically but they still don't take it for granted. Both still feel there is a dreamlike quality to the riches they enjoy and are determined that it won't end in a nightmare.

To that end, Wayne first knocked his gambling habit on the head after he lost £50,000 in a year while at his first club Everton. Then he joined the England squad and his gambling spiralled out of control as he allegedly ran up debts of £700,000.

He said: 'I did win three good sums but then I started losing and Sir Alex said to keep it in moderation or I could lose all my money.' It's advice Wayne has accepted – to this day both he and Coleen still pinch themselves over their luck.

She said: 'I'd never imagine I would end up living in a big house with all of this. Never imagine the car you drive and the stuff you can buy. Wayne thinks the same way as well. Sometimes he'll sit there and say, "I can't believe it". We don't take things for granted – or each other. If either of us did, we'd say something. That's the relationship. I'd be like, "Who do you think you are? You're Wayne, you know…" but I don't think I'd ever have to do that.'

But Wayne and Coleen's time together isn't always blissful. Again, like any couple, they bicker and row but she told *Hello* magazine: 'Wayne doesn't see himself as any kind of hero – and nor do I see him that way. If he's got a cob on I'll say to him, "Who do you think you are? Pelé?" It always makes him laugh.'

Coleen is still barely out of her teens and some of the criticism she has received in the media has reduced her to tears. At one point, headlines roared with allegations of Wayne's infidelity and ignorantly sneered at Coleen as a gold-digger for standing by him.

The beauty was in floods of tears before flying into a rage and fleeing home to her parents to try and sort out the mess. Later she told Wayne, 'One more girl and I'm gone' following a six hour meeting in which Coleen's parents Colette and Tony acted as peacemakers after dashing back from a holiday in Florida. During the emotionally charged meeting mum Colette had told the star, 'I love you like a son but you have got to stop hurting my daughter.'

Meanwhile Tony told the *Sunday Mirror*: 'Wayne and Coleen are trying to patch up their differences. You've got to take the good with the bad. Our relationship with Wayne's family is good – and it will stay that way.'

So, as the couple battled to save their relationship, Coleen was ignorantly accused of being a girl who hung on to Rooney for what was in his wallet and who would regret forgiving him. But she says she was made out to be somebody totally different to the person her friends and family know and, not surprisingly, it upset her. 'I'm like any girl my age' she said. 'I still cry if I get spots and like going out enjoying myself with my mates.'

Another shock headline, claiming that Wayne had slapped Coleen during a lovers' tiff in a nightclub, also left Coleen reeling. The allegation was later proved untrue – and Wayne was awarded £100,000 in compensation.

Even though Wayne has a sparky temper and an aggressive edge on the pitch, Coleen's own mum refused to believe that Wayne had hit her.

Furious Colette said: 'Wayne is one of the gentlest, sweetest people you could meet. We all have rows and that's all it was – a row. But I can assure you

Wayne would never lay a hand on Coleen. He hasn't got it in him.'

And Coleen's granddad Tommy added in an interview with the *Daily Star*: 'He's an absolutely smashing lad. We all love him. I can honestly say I have never seen them rowing and I see them all the time. They're so comfortable together. They make a great couple. As far as they're concerned the row is water under the bridge. It just does your head in when you hear about all the stuff made up about them. But it doesn't matter because at the end of the day they are really happy together.

'It makes you cross to read all the stuff written to knock them down. If only people could see them together, they'd know. We're all now just waiting for the big day. Everyone is hoping they can get it sorted this year.'

Coleen is insistent that the couple have weathered the storm of sex slur revelations about Wayne and come out stronger for it.

She says: 'Wayne is dead caring, he makes me feel special. He cheers me up with his funny sense of humour, he's a great mimic and he's always doing impressions of people off the telly. I love him to bits, I know he loves me and that won't change.'

Coleen has kept her feet on the ground thanks to keeping her true friends and family close but even today, she still finds Wayne's superstar status slightly surreal.

She said: 'I still find it hard to believe that my Wayne is the Wayne Rooney who gets his name chanted on the pitch. It's great when you walk into Old Trafford, all the fans chanting his name. I love it but I still find it overwhelming. Sometimes when I see him out on the pitch at Old Trafford with all those thousands of people screaming I think, "My God, look at all these people coming here to watch Wayne and the team."

'I often say to him, "What does it feel like to be out there?" Now and again he will stop and take it all in and he will say, "Did you hear them all shouting nice things?" and he will come home on a high.

'The fans play such a big part, that's what he always says, they are the ones who come and pay to see the team play and Wayne respects that, particularly the ones who travel away, he always says how great they are.'

By her own admission, Coleen isn't that knowledgeable on football. She only really enjoys watching when Wayne is playing and she doesn't like watching it on the television except perhaps if it's Manchester United or Liverpool. But, she says, 'Wayne knows I'm not that into football but he also knows I am his biggest fan. He is definitely The One.'

The couple have not yet set a date for their wedding but the pair have discussed detailed plans.

Said Coleen: 'We're even more in love than we ever were. Of course I'm looking forward to marrying Wayne. I am completely in love with him. My wedding will be the happiest day of my life. I'm always thinking about it, having ideas and stuff and talking to Wayne about it. We're fine together, we belong together and nothing is going to change that. He's the love of my life.'

Coleen knows that even though the couple hang out with millionaire mates and wear expensive designer gear, it's the everyday stuff they do together that keeps him at her side.

She says: 'You can have money and still be down-to-earth. It's really important to stay close to old family and friends. I even like going to Tesco. Okay, people stare at what we are buying, but it's really nice doing something domesticated together.'

While their wedding day may not yet be set, Coleen has already picked the names for the babies they plan to have. 'I would love to have a family,' she says. 'I wouldn't like to be old and lonely. My favourite name for a boy is Lucas. I love the name because it has so much meaning. It comes from the Latin word for light. I think it's lovely to choose names that have meaning – my favourite for a girl is

Ava. It means breath of life in Old English and waterfall in Persian.'

Coleen insists she and Wayne won't follow their pals the Beckhams by naming a child after the place it was conceived, like Brooklyn. Instead, she says she was inspired by the 'meaningful' name Tom Cruise and Katie Holmes have given their daughter. The Hollywood couple called her Suri, which is said to mean princess in Hebrew. Coleen told *The Sun*: 'I think that's such a lovely name too. All young girls have dreams about what they will call their kids one day.'

Meanwhile, Coleen is concentrating on supporting her Wayne, and planned to stand out in the crowd when she cheered on her man at the World Cup in 2006 by wearing a shirt emblazoned with his England number.

She explained: 'I was sent a World Cup kit including vests with Wayne's Number 9 on them in diamante. He certainly didn't miss me in the crowd!'

Coleen helped nurse Wayne back to health after his World Cup dreams seemed in tatters when he was stretchered off with a fracture in the fourth metatarsal on his right foot after a tackle by Chelsea full-back Paulo Ferreira in May 2006, a mere six weeks before the start of the World Cup.

Coleen was in tears as Wayne cried out and fell to

the ground writhing in agony. Doctors reckoned the injury would take six weeks to heal – and the couple even slept in an oxygen tent at their home to help Wayne recover in time.

Said Coleen: 'I was worried when I saw the look on Wayne's face as he went down. I was gutted for him, distraught. But my Wayne has always been a fighter. He's fit and a quick healer – we all prayed for him and the fans were brilliant with their support.'

Wayne's broken foot meant Coleen had to miss a pre-World Cup sunshine and shopping spree with England's glamorous wives and girlfriends at the five-star Vale Do Lobo resort on the Portuguese coast. While the players train, the girls can soak up the rays on a private beach, play tennis, shop at exclusive designer boutiques or chill out in the spa and pool.

But Coleen said: 'There's nowhere I'd rather be than at Wayne's side. I can't believe anybody would imagine otherwise.'

Whatever the truth may be about Rooney's visits to a brothel or flirtations with other girls, it's clear that the couple share a fiercely passionate friendship which will help them weather any storm.

Coleen believes in forgiveness and she is the only

person Wayne has confessed all to. He can only feel guilt at hurting the woman he loves yet the couple have remained together through thick and thin and all the mud-slinging.

They may be young, they may sometimes be silly but most of all they are truly in love. Anyone who doubts it may yet end up looking foolish.

CHAPTER FIVE

the big match

COLEEN, a pony-tailed, dark blonde girl with clear, cat-green eyes was just twelve years old when she first met Wayne. He was already a friend of her brother Anthony and had popped round to borrow a pair of shin pads. He was smitten with the girl from the moment he first saw her.

Says Wayne: 'I had to walk past Coleen's house every day to get to school. I didn't really know Coleen at that stage and I just used to hang around with other lads up the road. I liked her straight away and by the time I was fourteen I knew I fancied her. But Coleen wasn't really interested in boys. She was a goody who did her homework and all I was interested in was football.'

Coleen was a pupil at the strict, all-girls St John Bosco Roman Catholic School where Wayne's mum Jeanette worked as a part-time cleaner, and was a friend of Claire, the sister of one of the soccer star's favourite cousins, Thomas.

It was Thomas' dad – Wayne's uncle – Richie who owned the boxing gym where Wayne and his younger brothers Graham and John would often sit and watch football matches on the widescreen telly with their mates, including Coleen's brothers Anthony, and Joe.

Eight families from the close-knit Rooney and McLoughlin clan were neighbours on the Croxteth estate and the tentacles of their friendships often crossed. Coleen's parents lived a few minutes' walk around the corner from Wayne's family and, like Wayne Snr, her dad Tony had been a keen amateur boxer.

He helped Wayne's uncle Richie to run the boxing gym and had coached young Wayne there as a boy. The families shared in common an earnest Roman Catholic faith and a fierce desire to see their children succeed.

Wayne, a bashful lad, quiet and shy, was comfortable around Coleen. She was a no-nonsense girl who, like him, harboured a burning ambition. Since the age of six she had wanted to be an actress and, like him, was hard-working and wholly dedicated to her goal.

At school she recalls playing rounders, dabbling in athletics and swimming but never really excelling – 'I was good at backstroke, I should have gone to swimming club,' she told *You* magazine.

Academically, she held her own, gaining eleven GCSEs, but she wasn't as outstandingly clever as her younger brother Joe. 'He's got it, I had to work hard for it,' she confessed. She was, though, seen as responsible enough to be appointed deputy head girl of her Catholic girls' school.

The green buds of the couple's romance grew from a steady, innocent friendship, flourishing on the street corners of Croxteth before love begun to blossom. 'I can remember Wayne playing football in the street with my brothers,' says Coleen. 'I was only twelve when we first met and we were all just mates at first.'

As the afternoon light began to fade, Wayne would often ride out on his mountain bike to fetch paper-wrapped fries from the local chippie, returning to find Coleen sitting on a wall, watching as her brothers and their mates played soccer. He'd plonk himself down beside her, offering her chips with a nonchalance which belied his beating heart.

Says Wayne: 'I used to pull little stunts to try to get close to her because, until I know people, I can be quite shy. I desperately wanted to kiss her but I didn't know how. I remember once I pretended to have contact lenses that I couldn't get in my eyes and asked her to have a look and see if my eyes were okay, just to get her near to me.'

But Wayne was too shy to ask Coleen for a formal date.

As Coleen told *The Sun*: 'We used to spend hours just hanging around on the street corner, just talking to each other. At first, we were just mates but then we began to spend more time together and we became best friends – Wayne knows me better than anyone else.'

But she didn't know much about Wayne's main passion. Said Coleen: 'I never knew much about football until I met Wayne. He tried to explain the offside rule to me but I still don't understand it. Having said that, when the [2002] World Cup was on I would come down in the morning and my younger brothers Joe and Anthony would be watching the early morning games. I'd sit and watch with them because it was so exciting.'

Even so, Wayne's courage failed him every time the opportunity to ask for a date arose. Coleen was the girl-next-door he'd known since childhood, an ambitious, bright girl he counted as a trusted friend. He was uncertain whether the tender affection he felt towards her would be returned and, in a quandary, played the joker to try and gauge her feelings.

He said: 'I could never get the courage to ask her out properly or to kiss her. I used to try and ask but she wouldn't take it seriously. I invited her out on loads of dates – to the chippie, the pictures, I even promised to take her to Paris for Valentine's Day if she'd come on a date. She was gorgeous looking, had a great personality but she always thought I was teasing her because I did it in a jokey way.'

'Wayne can be quite a charmer,' explains Coleen. 'He used to chat me up by walking past my house and saying, "I've been waiting for your call" and he's just the same now. He's always skitting me.'

But underneath Wayne was a shy lad. The company of men was his comfort zone, either in the rough and tumble of his uncle's boxing gym, the light-hearted banter of the football changing room or on the testosterone-charged terraces at Everton. The acne-plagued awkwardness of youth, with limbs and hair sprouting, hormones running wild and emotions sky high, hadn't passed him by.

Wayne couldn't afford to be distracted from his soccer and, anyway, the cocky charm of the skirt-chaser wasn't in his nature. He was already too streetwise, too thoughtful, too self-aware for that, and counselled by parents who were only too familiar with the pitfalls of estate living.

Single motherhood was a fact of life on many of the estate's streets and within his own family. The potential for brief but catastrophic youthful fumblings to shatter dreams had also been carefully explained to Wayne at the Everton Academy. Avoiding temptation, confining conquest to the pitch, wised-up Wayne understood the value of cautious discipline.

Still, he couldn't get the girl who had captivated his heart out of his mind, his affected boyish indifference slowly evaporating as he came to recognise the unsettling feelings she evoked. Although he didn't know it yet, Wayne was falling in love.

Says Wayne: 'I was dead serious about dating her but I was too embarrassed to ask properly in case she turned me down or it spoiled our friendship. I felt shy about it and wasn't sure if she fancied me too or just liked me as a friend.'

It wasn't until Wayne turned knight in shining armour, riding to the rescue after spotting his princess in trouble, that he managed to win a date – and, then, only after enlisting the help of Claire, his cousin and Coleen's friend, even today.

He told me: 'My day came when the chain came off Coleen's bike. She was with my cousin Claire and I saw them trying to fix it. I was on my way home and stopped to help. I used it as an excuse to chat to Coleen, asking if I could borrow her video of *Grease* – I've always been a fan. I loved that movie and I knew she did too. When Coleen went inside to get the video, I grabbed Claire and asked her to get Coleen to come out on a date with me. By then, I was fed up of asking. But this time, Coleen said yes!'

The couple shyly walked across the street, Wayne's heart thudding as he knew his moment had come – he was going to steal a kiss off the girl he had adored for years. Carefully, he steered her towards the church, a place well known as a local lovers' lane where young sweethearts met for secret snogs.

Wayne explains: 'We went for a walk... we knew we were going to snog. My heart was going as fast as if I'd just played ninety minutes. I took her to the back of the church. It was the first kiss that ever mattered to me, she was special. I knew then that we were made for each other but I was lost for words. Coleen did most of the talking – I think she was shocked at what a fantastic kisser I was!

'I walked her home and I phoned her as soon as I got in and asked her for a proper date. The next day, we planned to go out. I'd arranged to meet my friends in town and I was so excited I bought a whole new outfit – a green jumper, jeans and brown shoes.'

The couple went to the Showcase Cinema, a frayed, old-fashioned picture house just a short stroll from their homes, to see *Austin Powers: International Man of Mystery*, followed by cheeseburger and chips at a fast-food restaurant close by. It was their first proper, unchaperoned date and Wayne walked her home, a shy acknowledgement between them that, now, they were officially an item.

'We realised we liked each other more than just mates,' is how Coleen puts it. 'When I first started seeing him, I was a bit nervous and we kept it secret. I never told my dad if I kissed a lad, he is quite protective and really strict. I was unsure how he would react to me having a boyfriend.'

Wayne was formally introduced to Coleen's family at a christening gathering for her cousin's baby. Says Coleen: 'Wayne wore jeans and a shirt – everybody loved him. I expected my dad to be more protective but he was quite relaxed because Wayne had been coming round so much and he knew his dad from boxing. They got on brilliantly.'

He was just sixteen, earning £90 a week at Everton, when he hung up his De La Salle school uniform for the last time at Easter.

Coleen had celebrated her sixteenth birthday on 3 April 2002, around the same time that Wayne has left school. So certain was he that she was to remain a permanent fixture in his life, he'd even had her name tattooed on his right shoulder. 'When he first rolled up his sleeve and showed me I was really proud,' recalled Coleen.

Again, he'd taken her to the cinema before they enjoyed her birthday outing to Liverpool's trendy 051 club – Wayne sipping shandy while she stuck to Coke – before taking a taxi back and lingering by the wall near her home, chatting amiably and excitedly about Wayne's prospects, until the front door opened and her mum called her in.

Coleen's parents were strict about time-keeping, anxious that she should prepare for the exacting A-levels she was due to begin at St John Bosco sixth-form in September, and determined that, what might be no more than a fleeting teenage infatuation, should not distract their clever daughter from her studies.

But Wayne already knew Coleen was the girl for him. He says: 'I stopped going out with my mates as much, although I still played football before I saw her every night! I just wanted to be with her. She was my best friend, I loved her and I loved being around her.'

As Wayne wandered slowly home, his mind quietly ticking over, he felt a bubble of happiness well inside and smiled – he knew Coleen was the girl he wanted to marry. It was just a matter of time before he'd let her know. It never once occurred to him that the whole world would want to know too.

The coals of the sweethearts' passion were ignited but their romance was forced to slow burn as Wayne's meteoric rise to stardom took off. And the moment when Wayne would shake the football world to its foundations and become a global soccer star, was just around the corner. Destiny would come knocking, first in the momentous signing for his beloved Everton and then, with fairytale unreality, in the form of England manager Sven-Goran Eriksson.

After a string of sensational performances for the youth team, Wayne was instantly promoted to Everton's first team squad and handed the Number 18 shirt previously sported by Paul Gascoigne, he took just weeks to smash his way into the club's record books. On 24 September 2002, in a bitterly contested match against Wrexham, the teenage powerhouse became Everton's youngest ever scorer, sent on as a substitute to belt home two astonishing goals in the Worthington Cup win.

But it was his spectacular last-minute goal against Arsenal in a Premiership match at Goodison Park a month later which left the football world open-mouthed, drooling at the sheer, audacious brilliance of the boy, a boy still five days short of his seventeenth birthday.

It was a goal which saw world-class keeper David Seaman, the England squad's safe pair of hands, left sitting helplessly on his backside – and saw Rooney become the Premiership's youngest ever scorer.

On 24 October, his seventeenth birthday, he became a fully fledged member of the Everton elite, signing his first professional contract and becoming one of the richest youngsters in world football, earning up to £18,000 a week, including bonuses.

The three-year deal – the maximum length of time for a seventeen year old – made him the highest paid teenager in Everton's history, earning the kind of mind-boggling money each week that those from his home turf in Croxteth rarely saw in a year. A £2 million endorsement deal with Nike plopped through the letterbox just weeks later, signed with a trembling flourish by the disbelieving lad.

With a maturity beyond their years, both Wayne and Coleen recognised their ambitions would necessitate sacrifices, a fact which became glaringly obvious when Wayne's starburst talent catapulted him into the spotlight on the world stage.

For instance, some months later, while he dazzled on the pitch in England's 2-0 win over Turkey in England's Euro 2004 qualifier, Coleen remained at home to star as Fat Sam in her school's production of *Bugsy Malone* and, earlier, had stayed behind an extra day to sit an English exam while Wayne flew out to join the squad at Spain's La Manga camp for pre-season training.

But that was in the future. Meanwhile, an awe-inspiring legend was being carved on the hallowed pitches of England's Premiership clubs – and, starting on 12 February 2003, the whole world would hear the story.

Knock, knock…

Who's there?

Sven….

His debut match against Australia at Upton Park that month was a humiliating defeat for England, a 3-1 scoreline to the Socceroos which sent English hearts plummeting, especially since the Three Lions had been odds-on favourites to win.

But a hero emerged from the ashes of that defeat – Rooney, England's youngest ever player at the age of 17 years and 111 days, had outperformed some of the nation's biggest soccer names. He'd played alongside his heroes, men he'd cheered wildly as a schoolboy, sitting in the front room of his gran's council house, willing England to victory.

His name was on everyone's lips. Suddenly, the world was his oyster, people clamouring to congratulate and celebrate with the new star. But there was just one place he wanted to be – back on the proud-as-punch streets of Croxteth, with the girl he loved.

Said Coleen: 'When Wayne scored in matches I had to look back and think, "That's my Wayne, the man I love." I could hardly believe it was my boyfriend. It didn't seem real. Afterwards, when I was on my own and I read about the goals in the newspapers, I got a huge surge of love and pride and I still do.'

The thrill of the record-breaking game still coursing through his veins, Wayne dashed back to share his first moments of glory with Coleen and was dropped off at her parents' home by a friend – an England star he may have been, but he still hadn't passed his driving test.

Later, as twilight blanketed the ragged Croxteth skyline, Wayne shared a bag of chips, a bottle of Coke and a kickabout in the street with his mates, just an ordinary evening for the extraordinary boy who had the world at his feet.

It would be the last time he'd need to buy his own Coke – within weeks Rooney had signed up with Coleen to front a £500,000 advertising campaign with the fizzy drinks giant, a team effort like Posh and Becks before them.

And just a month later the lad who had worn hand-me-down trainers was revelling in the luxurious surrounds of the England training camp at La Manga, where the team had gone to prepare for the 2004 European Championship qualifiers. It was a million miles from the caravan in a Welsh holiday park near Rhyl where he'd spent childhood holidays with his cousins, the boys booting their way to glory on a tufted square of sun-baked grass which served as their stadium.

La Manga was a name Wayne knew, famous as the base for England's pre-season training and frequently linked in newspaper headlines with tales of drunken antics and high jinks among the pampered players. And here he was, about to join the serried ranks of England shirts at the Spanish resort, his dream of playing in the Euro 2004 qualifiers just a few weeks from becoming reality.

La Manga, a five-star resort where the scent of money wafts lazily across the manicured lawns, spoke of exotic luxuries Wayne had only ever brushed up against in the pages of glossy magazines, left carelessly discarded in the players' lounge at Everton for others to flick through aimlessly.

It held few mysteries, though. He'd been carefully coached from an early age by the team at Everton's Academy and taken under the wing of Alan Stubbs, now 33, a senior club player, who'd ensured the boy from the back streets was well steeped in the polish which would help him blend in.

But for Coleen, still every inch a schoolgirl, the very thought of setting foot in the place was enough to stir the kind of frantic anxiety any woman feels on her first foray into unknown sophistication, never mind a sixth-form student from the tough streets of Croxteth. 'I didn't know what to expect, I was dead scared and nervous,' she says.

The couple's relationship was now a firm fixture. Wayne had been welcomed into Coleen's family, staying at their home overnight to share tender moments with his girl.

He says: 'Coleen had a TV and video in her bedroom and we'd go upstairs together to watch things like *Grease* or *Armageddon*. I remember I told Coleen I loved her first. We were watching *Pearl Harbor*, sitting on the sofa at her house. I just told her I loved her. I think the film was a bit of an emotional one and it just came over me.

'Even when I used to go home, which was just down the road, I'd phone her as soon as I got in the door to tell her I was back. Then I'd text her to tell her I loved her, and I'd often pick her up from school.'

The rock solid relationship met with the approval of Coleen's mum and dad. They recognised Wayne's serious intent – and their daughter's love for him –

and agreed to allow Coleen to make her first trip alone with Wayne to La Manga.

It would be the first time she had flown alone – Coleen had to sit an English exam on the day the squad flew out, joining her hero a day later. And she was petrified! She remembers: 'I rang Wayne and asked him to find out what kind of clothes the women were wearing. I told him to look when they came down for breakfast, but he told me everyone had eaten in their rooms. I was really worried I would take the wrong clothes or not know what to do.'

Just a few months earlier, she'd decked herself out in a simple powder-blue top and white jeans to celebrate her seventeenth birthday with Wayne at the Kung Fu Chinese restaurant in St Helens, five miles away from the house she still shared with her parents. The couple had feasted on vegetable spring rolls, mixed vegetable chow mein and sweet and sour chicken with fried rice, washed down with Coke, before Wayne paid the £40 bill.

Later, delighted Coleen unwrapped her sweetheart's gift to her, a £6,000 Marc Jacobs watch, soon to be replaced that Christmas with an £18,000 diamond-encrusted platinum Rolex, *de rigeur* amongst the glitterati at La Manga.

But despite that, with her flat, black shoes, short socks, lumpy padded anorak and skin devoid of make up, Coleen, a rucksack slung across her shoulders, was still the kind of everyday girl who could be spotted at bus stops across the nation.

She was relying on her man to come up with the vital information on the wardrobe requirements. But, like a typical bloke, Wayne couldn't understand what all the fuss was about. Clad casually in T-shirt and shorts as he roamed the upmarket resort, he still hadn't completed his spy mission by the time a nerve-wracked Coleen was boarding her plane from Britain.

Says Coleen: 'When I got to the airport, I rang him again to find out and he still didn't know. Luckily, when I arrived I had bought the right clothes.'

A resourceful girl, Coleen, like her friends, had spent many hours on dreary, rainy days poring over pictures of the high-maintenance women often found draped on the arms of footballers and pop stars. An express shopping trip with her mum around the designer stores of Manchester – a short hop from Liverpool and boasting a posh Harvey Nichol's – secured the glitzy dresses, sunglasses and trendy red Burberry bikini which would see her elevated to covergirl status from the minute she touched down on her sun lounger.

She says: 'My mum rang me to tell me there were pictures of me all over the newspapers. I couldn't believe it – I was dead worried what I looked like in my bikini!'

She needn't have worried. The girl Wayne affectionately called Babe looked gorgeous, a refreshing change from the sleekly expensive artifice surrounding her, and was soon the tabloid's darling, her natural curves, dewy young skin and innocent charm elbowing Victoria Beckham off the front pages.

At first, naturally, Coleen was overawed by the world-famous celebrities around her. Surreally, people she'd only ever seen in pictures sat beside her at breakfast, chattering with their families about plans for the day over freshly baked croissants, at ease and at home in the plush surroundings.

Liverpool's striker Michael Owen, his baby daughter Gemma nestled in his arms, lounged in the sun with his partner Louise Bonsall, sharing a joke with Wayne. Steven Gerrard, also a hero-worshipped Red, and his stunning girlfriend Alex, soaked up the 80F heat nearby, teasing the couple with Scouse humour and beginning a bond, which would later see him become a pal to Rooney, as the lad sweltered under the unwavering glare of the spotlight.

Queen bee Victoria Beckham offered the hand of friendship, inviting Coleen to spend the day with the girls while the boys sloped off for a game of golf, a first for Wayne but, inevitably, not a last, or to challenge each other at go-karting.

Soon, Coleen was gossiping away with the rest of them, relaxed in sleeveless T-shirt – the royal blue of Everton, of course – and grey camouflage shorts as she absorbed the buzz of conversation around her.

'Victoria was chatting away, she was lovely,' says Coleen, 'but I mostly hung out with Steven Gerrard, Jamie Carragher and Michael Owen and their girlfriends because we're all from Liverpool. I would like a little of what Victoria has, her clothes and look,' adds Coleen, 'but I don't see her as someone to look up to because I think everyone should be their own person.'

Alone, at night, she snuggled up with Wayne to watch *Only Fools and Horses* on a DVD player, dissecting the day before joining their new found celebrity friends at dinner.

It was the stuff dreams are made of, the dreams of little boys and girls who weave feverish fantasies as they fall into slumber, knowing they'll never likely come true. But, for the very lucky, talented and select few, those dreams do come true.

'I have to pinch myself to believe what's happened to Wayne,' says Coleen, 'but nobody deserves it more. He's always worked dead hard and he has a brilliant talent. I'm so proud of him.'

The couple's love affair found breathing space on their first holiday alone in 2003, an eye-opening adventure in America's Miami, lazing on the beach and soaking up the atmosphere in one of the USA's most celebrated playgrounds. It was there, during blissful sun-soaked days, that love blossomed from courtship to commitment. The rosy hue of a future marriage hung in the air and, just a week later, the couple joined both their families in the smart Mexican resort of Cancun.

Says Wayne: 'It was a dream holiday compared to those when I was little, but we were young and thought we might be bored on our own, so we invited our parents to join us in Mexico. We had a villa and we asked Coleen's dad if we could share a room. Coleen was nervous asking her dad, but it was all right.

'I was a bit awkward at first, too. I didn't know what her dad was going to come out with, because he has a dry sense of humour. My parents came as well and they didn't mind at all. They didn't give us the speech about safe sex, we were old enough to know about that. Coleen's mum had chatted to her about it, but not in a big lecture kind of way. We knew we wanted to be together and stay together.'

But, while affairs of the heart were rapidly fermenting, the siren song of Wayne's first love was calling and, on 6 September 2003 he answered with a passion which took the nation's breath away. Another record toppled as Wayne became the youngest England player ever to score in a full international, netting the first goal in a 2–1 Euro 2004 qualifier against Macedonia in September.

Coleen, who had just returned to school to start her A-levels, had to be content with watching her lover shoot his way to victory on the TV at home. 'My whole family were at the house to watch the game,' she says. 'I rang Wayne the day before and said to him, 'Are you going to score for me today?' and he said, "Yes!" When the goal went in, I couldn't believe it. I was rooted to the spot for a moment, I didn't think or do anything. Then, when it sank in, I jumped out of my chair and started screaming and cheering. My dad's a Liverpool supporter but the whole family were leaping around and hugging each other. I was so dead proud of him.'

Wayne later admitted he was just as gobsmacked, so blinded by euphoria that he didn't know what to do or where to run to after he'd scored!

Rooney may have been just seventeen years old but, with the same certainty that had directed his boots, he knew where his romantic heart lay and, just a month later, the soccer star formally proposed to his sweetheart… on the forecourt of a BP garage!

'I had the ring made to my design,' said Wayne. 'It's platinum and diamond, I know what Coleen likes. Coleen had tried to interfere but she made it too complicated! I'd picked it up from the jeweller and told her we were going out for a Chinese meal, but we stopped at a BP petrol station to get money from the cashpoint. When Coleen was getting the cash, I got the box out of my pocket and had it open. She got back into the car and I asked, "Will you marry me?"

'She was a bit emotional, she said "Yes" and we had a bit of a hug. Asking Coleen to marry me was worse than walking out for England. We didn't bother going for that meal. We rang Coleen's mum and told her to get the dinner on and went back to watch *EastEnders*. Coleen couldn't wait to get back and show everybody her ring. She loved it. When we got there, her mum had put candles on the table and all. It was really special.

The couple had already discussed marriage, but Wayne wanted to go the whole hog and follow the traditional route of asking Coleen's dad for his daughter's hand in marriage.

He said: 'We'd already discussed getting married a few months earlier. We knew we were only young but Coleen talked to her mum and she was happy for us. So were my parents when we spoke to them, too. But I was determined to ask her dad properly.'

But, as ever where Coleen was concerned, determined Wayne's nerves got the better of him on the night as he sat anxiously looking for an opportunity to ask Tony for his daughter's hand in marriage. Tony was only too aware of what Wayne was there for – and enjoyed every moment of watching his discomfort!

Said Wayne: 'I'll never forget the night. We were all sat in the living room watching TV and her dad already knew what was on my mind because her mum had told him. Eventually, after four hours of awkward silence, he finally said to me, "Haven't you got something to say to me Wayne?"

'And I blurted out, "Can I marry your daughter please?" Then he gave me a big lecture and said, "If you love each other, I give my blessing."

'Then he told me to look after her but said it was two people from the same area who loved each other and he knew it was right. Finally, he shook my hand and her mum started to cry.'

Even better, just a few weeks before receiving permission from Coleen's dad, Wayne had passed his driving test – on his third attempt – and the couple could seek the privacy they craved away from the bright lights of Liverpool.

Said Coleen: 'If we went out for dinner or out shopping we got a lot of people coming up to us. So we mostly went to the cinema because it was dark and no one could see who Wayne was. Even now, we do our shopping at Tesco at 10 p.m. because we're less likely to see many people.

'When Wayne passed his driving test, it made things a lot easier.

'He was very nervous when he proposed. People think we are too young but I don't think we are. It is up to the individual… I know the time is right. It's not up to anyone else. He is the person I love and want to stay with for the rest of my life. I want his children, we want a boy and a girl.

'But we haven't set a date yet. I actually feel too young to do that. I want it to be beautiful and really well planned. A wedding only comes once so I want it to be dead special. We can be engaged for years so there's plenty of time to make wedding plans.'

Wayne, unafraid to wear his heart on his sleeve, said simply, 'She's a nice girl to be around and I wanted to make sure I keep her around.'

Just a few weeks later, Wayne moved in with Coleen's parents after buying his own mum and dad a £470,000 home in Liverpool's upmarket West Derby. He explains: 'Mum and dad were moving and getting their house sorted so I moved in with Coleen's parents. I was virtually living there anyway – I spent most evenings with Coleen at her house.'

By November 2003, the couple were enjoying the kind of high-profile celebrity lifestyle common amongst the footballing elite, canoodling in a VIP area at a Beyonce Knowles concert and later, Coleen waltzing down the catwalk in a red mini-dress, raising cash at a charity fashion show.

Within a few weeks, she'd signed up with Wayne's influential agent Paul Stretford, landed a small part in Chester-based soap *Hollyoaks* and quit her A-level studies. 'I just felt doing A-levels wasn't right for me,' said Coleen. 'It was difficult with all the attention I was getting and I was being offered acting parts but I couldn't take them because of my schoolwork. I'd like to go to drama school, maybe to university, but there's plenty of time to do that.'

The lovebirds finally spent their first night alone on Valentine's Day, 2004, enjoying chocolates and champagne at Liverpool's Marriott Hotel, a lavishly restored art deco building which was formerly an old-fashioned airport terminal.

Says Wayne: 'We were going to a party and, halfway through the night, I asked Coleen, "Should I phone your dad and ask if we can stay out?" He said "Yes" so I booked a room at the Marriot Hotel in Liverpool. We arrived at about 1 a.m. and there was champagne and chocolates already there. It was a fantastic night, our first full night completely alone together.'

Just a month later, the couple would leave behind the streets of Croxteth to move into their new £1.3 million mansion in Formby, a 20-minute drive from the council estate which had spawned their love – but a million miles away in riches.

CHAPTER SIX
life's a dream

EVEN as a child, Coleen knew what she wanted from life. While others at her school wrote down their wishes for jobs as lawyers, nurses or doctors, her dream was prophetic: to be rich and live a life of luxury.

She hoped to achieve her aim with an acting career. Instead, she was wrenched from her studies after the spotlight of publicity arising from her romance with Wayne, became too hot to handle.

She was just a simple schoolgirl, more used to reading about celebrities in glossy magazines than appearing in their pages. But suddenly, she was pursued every moment by photographers and journalists desperate for a scoop on the girl who had won the heart of Britain's hottest football prospect since George Best forged a path to glory.

It was intense and relentless and Wayne was determined to protect his girl, moving her from the terraced home she shared with her parents to a five bedroom mansion, in Liverpool's posh Formby while he was still at Everton.

For Coleen, a girl who had never spent more than a few days away from the familiar pock-marked streets of Croxteth, the dramatic change in lifestyle proved difficult to come to terms with.

Says Wayne: 'Coleen went to see the house first and loved it, so then we went together and, when I saw it, I knew it was the place for us. But, when we first moved in, it was weird, so big and empty. I remember Coleen's mum crying because she was going to miss her so much but I had always wanted a house of my own and I wanted Coleen to live with me, where she would be safe and I could look out for her.

'It wasn't difficult for me, because I was used to going away from my family for training and to play in competitions and staying in hotels. But it was a lot for Coleen to cope with. She was just eighteen and to have a house like ours of her own was a lot on her shoulders.'

Homesick Coleen was so intimidated by the huge

house that she couldn't even go up to bed alone, where she found the silence unnerving.

Said Wayne: 'Coleen couldn't sleep on her own. Where we lived before, her house was on a main road and there was always the noise of traffic, but when we moved, everything was very quiet, you could hear a pin drop. She got scared, so we got a dog, a chow called Fizz. I would take Coleen up to bed, and watch a DVD until she fell asleep.'

Coleen and Wayne are each the crutch on which each other leans. They may be rich beyond most of our wildest dreams, but it doesn't stop them feeling the same way and nor does it prevent them from behaving like the youngsters they are.

Said Coleen: 'Some people are jealous of our relationship and want to knock us down all the time. I think they are the people who aren't content with their own lives. But it has been hard. I cried for two weeks when we moved into our first house in Liverpool and that was just 25 minutes away from my mum. Then when Wayne moved to Manchester United I thought that was a big move. Now I realise it's only 45 minutes away.

'I love to have my friends and family around me, I know I can count on them, especially when horrible things are being said about me.'

Despite the emotional wrench Coleen, still just

eighteen, was determined to make the house a home for the man she loved, a sanctuary from the adulation – and criticism – that followed his every move.

'It was my priority, to make us a home,' said Coleen. 'We didn't have much time to settle into the house, what with training for the Euro 2004 tournament and then going to the tournament itself. I had it done in creams and beiges, it was quite plain and calm.'

In the dining room a vast picture of Wayne scoring his first goal for England – against Macedonia in September 2003 – took pride of place across one wall. It was his most treasured possession. All the England players and staff had signed it, including Steven Gerrard who put 'well done, ugly arse'.

But Wayne and Coleen had barely time to buy a sofa before they were on the move again – he to Manchester United with Coleen by his side.

It was a move which saw Wayne vilified on Merseyside, with graffiti sprawled across walls saying, 'Die Rooney Die', and his family receiving hate mail and telephone calls. Furious Everton fans believed he had betrayed the club and poured bile on the young Rooney who was even said to have received death threats. When the couple visited Coleen's family's home they were greeted by painted slogans – 'Rooney judas' and 'Rooney scum'.

An amazing security blitz was put in place to protect the couple, with two SAS-trained minders watching their backs at all times as well as a personal bodyguard for Wayne. It meant the couple had to leave their Formby home and move to a safe house near the club's boss Sir Alex Ferguson, amidst fears of kidnap attempts.

Today, Wayne and Coleen have moved both sets of their parents to the outskirts of Liverpool, near West Derby, where they have state of-the-art security.

The couple coped with the extraordinary reaction of Everton fans by keeping their heads low and taking counsel from Sir Alex Ferguson, known as a no-nonsense father figure.

A further example of the downside of fame and riches, and the spite in brings out in some people came in May 2006, when Coleen's family discovered vandals had targeted their cars.

Says Coleen: 'Our family cars were vandalised outside my mum and dad's house in May. Someone smashed three cars, including the people carrier we used to drive my disabled sister Rosie around. It's ridiculous behaviour and shows a great deal of disrespect. How would they feel if someone had done that to their car? As it was, we had no transport for Rosie for 24 hours while it was fixed – what if she'd had to go into hospital suddenly?

'It's astonishing how disrespectfully some people behave – maybe it is jealousy. We have accepted over the years that there is a certain amount of jealousy but this is way over the top. It's inexcusable.'

The attack caused thousands of pounds worth of damage to the vehicles parked outside the McLoughlins' home. Coleen's parents were woken at 4 a.m. by the sound of a car alarm. They discovered that the people carrier had been trashed along with Wayne's £26,000 Volkswagen Golf R32 and another Golf belonging to Coleen's brother Joe.

They dialled 999 and Tony rushed downstairs. All he saw was the yobs' black car, possibly a Vauxhall Corsa, vanishing into the distance.

Tony added: 'All kinds of things have happened since Wayne and Coleen became famous. We have had to change our phone number three times because we were getting malicious calls. And we get a lot of hate mail. We don't read it – it goes straight in the bin. All the cars have had eggs smashed over them.

'But to attack Rosie's car and smash the windows is beyond belief. These people have gone too far. They are below contempt. It was pure, mindless vandalism.'

Coleen's mum Colette wept as she described how the thugs had taken a hammer to the specially adapted Vauxhall Zafira, which takes Rosie to hospital and respite care.

She said: 'I'm heartbroken. It's our baby's car, Rosie has a life-threatening condition. We need that car to get her around. I can understand the resentment about Wayne. But to do this to our severely handicapped baby's car is despicable, just pure evil.'

Wayne's family have also suffered from the spite of vandals. Thugs twice slashed the tyres on the family's new Ford Galaxy people carrier in one week and their home was later attacked with a paintball gun.

Three pellets filled with green paint were fired at their home, one hitting the brickwork and two the upper window where an Everton pennant fluttered in the wind. A fourth pellet hit the family car. The culprits were suspected to be rival Liverpool fans but Wayne's dad was reluctant to go to the police.

He said: 'We don't know why people are doing it. I think maybe they are jealous. We didn't go to the police because there's nothing they can do.'

Following the backlash of Wayne's controversial move to Manchester United, Wayne and Coleen went home hunting again, settling on a £3.5 million, six-bedroom pile in the coveted Prestbury area of Cheshire to be made over to their own specifications. The couple held on to the house in Formby as an investment property.

Coleen hired top interior designer Dawn Ward – who charges a cool £150,000 for her efforts and is wed to Sheffield United striker Ashley Ward – to make sure there were no fashion blunders like those to be found in her old wardrobe. She also splashed out £1.2 million on furnishings, making sure every detail of the couple's new home was the epitome of good taste.

Plans for the sprawling estate – including acres of woodland – showed the house would boast a 20-seat cinema, a games room big enough to take a full-size snooker table, a piano room, a hairdressing and beauty salon and even a £12,000 spray tanning booth.

All six of the new bedrooms have Bang & Olufsen plasma TV and sound systems, costing around £5,800 each, as well as en-suite wetrooms – posh bathrooms where you can spray water around to your heart's content without worrying about getting the floor wet.

The master bedroom has his and hers walk in dressing rooms and a balcony, so they can sit and admire their landscaped grounds.

There is also an indoor heated pool with steam room and a recessed jacuzzi spa bath finished with carved wood mouldings at a cost of around £5,000. Above the pool is a gallery which incorporates a state-of-the-art gym. The walls and floor are fully tiled with limestone and a huge £13,000 plasma screen TV dominates the room.

Plans showed that the kitchen has Italian marble

worktops, which Coleen insisted on, solid wood units by Clive Christian costing £60,000 and expensive imported chrome taps and sinks. Appliances include a fridge-freezer made by Sub-zero, which can cost up to £8,000 and a wine-cooler by the same firm which sells for around £6,000. A £5,000 cooking range from sought-after US brand Wolf dominates the room.

Downstairs, which includes a dining room panelled in oak, there are carved marble fireplaces and, because Coleen hates radiators, everywhere has underfloor heating. All the living areas have oak floors adorned with hand-made rugs and the Clive Christian theme is continued with a selection of his furniture.

The plans also included a large wooden conservatory which opens out on to gardens at the rear. Flanking the house is a triple garage for the couple's motors – Coleen drives a Mercedes convertible and BMW M3, and a £30,000 Audi TT Roadster, £50,000 Cadillac Escalade, a £25,000 Chrysler and a £67,000 Porsche 911 make up the couple's collection.

The imposing entrance is adorned with pillars with another balcony above and at least twenty windows along the front elevation alone. Once inside, guests can hang up their coats in the cloakroom, which doubles up as a downstairs loo.

The house also has four staircases and each bedroom has an en-suite bathroom and almost all have their own dressing rooms, too. The master bedroom, a short walk via the massive master dressing room, features his and hers sinks and toilets. But, should the couple prefer a moment of privacy, there are eight further toilets at their disposal.

Said Coleen: 'There's so much to do and we know we are lucky but it means we haven't had time to even think about having a wedding yet.'

And Dawn added: 'They are not daft and they know what they want. They have a lot of money but they have a lot of good people around them and know how to spend it correctly. Never under-estimate footballers or their wives.'

The house, with its £120 rolls of wallpaper, was immediately dubbed 'Waynesor Castle' – and hasn't always proved a success with the neighbours who have made complaints that the pile is 'garish' and out of keeping with the local area.

But *Elle Deco* editor Rachel Loos says: 'It sounds like the most wonderful girlie fantasy. I wonder whether the salon has a nail bar and whether she will be inviting her friends round to try it out? I think I would. She has the money, or at least he has the money and she can spend it and there's no product or finish that's beyond her pocket.

'But the art of making a home isn't just about spending as much money as you possibly can. I have been into houses that had clearly had millions spent on them but the atmosphere inside made you want to walk straight out again. A lot of this kind of interior design is about making a statement, not so much "This is the style I like," as "This is what I can afford."

'Of course, you can't spend that kind of money on a house and then not make sure plenty of people see it. Then we'll know whether she's managed to put the warmth of a real home into it, or whether it gives the impression of being a mishmash of high price tags thrown together. The whole point is to avoid being derided as a home-maker with more money than taste.'

But, again, the couple's magnificent home drew the derision of middle-class snobs. The *Observer*'s David Aaronovitch said: 'We had the *Daily Mail* misdelivered to our house. Inside, over two whole pages, was an article assisted by a large cutaway illustration, about the new house being built by Wayne and Coleen.

'Two whole pages of sneering. So why the hatred? One answer is, of course, material envy, a constant in Britain. If the couple were Americans they would be celebrated but there is an element in the British psyche which is suspicious of success, as though it breaches some kind of national solidarity. It marks out too great a difference. Like children "showing off", it is somehow an affront to everyone else.'

With the new home taking upwards of a year to build, the couple now split their time between Wilmslow and Prestbury, often staying with Coleen's parents and enjoying her mum's home cooking back on the streets of Croxteth.

Said Coleen: 'My mum is a brilliant cook.' And it's a skill Coleen is hoping to emulate – she plans to take cookery lessons and has even spoken to top TV chef Antony Worrall Thompson about the possibility of training with him, to impress those invited to dinner in the couple's oak-panelled dining room.

'I like where we live now, between Liverpool and Manchester,' continued Coleen. 'It is nice and close to my family and friends and suits me fine. I don't think I would like to live abroad like David and Victoria. I wouldn't like to be too far away, I've always been a homebird and need familiar people and things around me.'

The couple also bought a £3-million penthouse in Manchester's prestigious Beetham Towers as an investment property – their neighbours include *X Factor* winner Shayne Ward – and looked for a palatial holiday home in Abu Dhabi.

They fell in love with Dubai – the Arabian

playground of the rich and famous – when they first holidayed there in 2004 but, on a girlie trip in March 2006 with her best friend and Wayne's cousin Claire, Coleen came home complaining that they had been followed wherever they went.

Wayne has now instructed property developers to find them a luxurious villa away from the tourist crowds, a few miles down the beaten track at Abu Dhabi where they can enjoy their privacy and are less likely to be spotted.

And he has also bought a box at Manchester's MEN arena where Coleen and her pals can watch some of the biggest names in pop perform without being pestered. Wayne shelled out for the Arena's top hospitality package, typically costing £20,000, so he can also take music-mad Coleen to all the gigs she fancies.

The private suite comes with a balcony over-looking the stage where the couple have already enjoyed seeing the likes of Blue, Avril Lavigne, Madonna, Beyonce and Kylie Minogue. The lovebirds enjoy a five-star pre-gig dinner and a waiter serves them throughout the show. 'He likes to spoil me,' Coleen said with a shy smile.

He certainly does – Coleen's jewellery collection includes a £10,000 Jacob & Co watch, her £25,000 Tiffany engagement ring and a £1 million diamond necklace, plus countless bracelets, earrings and other diamond-encrusted watches.

For Christmas Wayne pushed the boat out when the only gift Coleen could think of wanting was a Fendi bag. But Wayne upped the ante, ordering custom-made versions of his babe's favourite bags in seven colours directly from the Italian fashion house. And he asked for them to be personalised with diamonds for his fiancée. Each lavish bag cost Wayne more than £7,000 – the girlie present to end all others.

Coleen was delighted: 'I couldn't think of anything else I wanted apart from Fendi bags in every single colour. They're just perfect.'

But Coleen does worry that she is perceived as spoilt, having all the gifts lavished upon her. 'I hate it when the newspapers say Wayne pays for everything,' she explains. 'I have my own money from working now and he doesn't always pay. He used to tell me to forget about it, that people were just jealous, but it was hard. And, although I'm more confident now and I realise I've got to take the good with the bad, it still does annoy me when they go on about it.

'It's difficult for me, especially with the paparazzi. Sometimes I get angry and start shouting if they're just in my face. But sometimes I just think it's their job and I should feel honoured that they want my picture.'

Coleen even has her own personal shopper at Harvey Nichols' in the city, where she also has her own suite. It comes complete with plasma screens and changing rooms the size of a Chelsea apartment. It's situated on the second floor and features Coleen's favourite Missoni label – a scarf alone will set you back £60. There are never more than two shoppers on the floor at the same time, and shower facilities are provided if she needs to cool down after a mammoth spending spree on her credit card, bearing a three crowns motif.

For anyone in doubt, this is the insignia of Coutts and Co, The Queen's bankers, where in order to be taken on as a customer you need to have at least £500,000.

The minted duo are even following in the Beckhams' footsteps by designing their own coat of arms. They are spending £3,000 on the heraldic crest and Coleen wants it to reflect her love of shopping and her sweet tooth. She said: 'It will have a Chloe bag and shoes on it. And some Maltesers – my favourites.'

The couple's childhood holidays to Spanish apartments on the Costa del Sol or to a caravan park in Wales are no more than fond memories now, replaced by frolicking on white-sand beaches on lavish holidays to luxury resorts. The couple enjoy several holidays a year – Coleen often pops off for a girlie break without Wayne – which are a far cry from the penny-pinched holidays they spent as children.

Barbados – where the couple stayed at the swanky, £2,500 a night Sandy Lane hotel – has become a favourite, along with Dubai, Mallorca, America and Mexico.

It's the stuff long-cherished dreams are made of, the kind of lottery winner lifestyle which prompts millions to buy a £1 ticket each week in the hope that they might live it. But although they hobnob with the rich and famous Coleen still prefers her down-to-earth pals.

She says: 'We all used to sit around gossiping about what was in the magazines and tearing celebrities apart and we still do it – even though other people do it to me! Nothing has changed.'

Coleen has appeared in the pages of *Hello!*, *Company* and *Cosmopolitan* to name but a few and says, 'I always get the view of my mates on what I look like – I know they will tell me the truth. I only really see the other soccer stars' wives and girlfriends on match days. I tend to hang out with my old friends more, because I've known them for ages and they're a close group.'

Coleen also knows she can rely on her pals to look out for her when she needs to let her hair down. Sometimes a girl just needs to drown her sorrows, especially when her fiancé is laid up at home with a crocked foot.

Coleen was spotted looking the worse for wear in the early hours in May 2006, after a night spent knocking back champagne. The evening started at the launch of a new LG mobile phone, called The Chocolate, at plush Sketch bar in London's Mayfair. Then, after calling Wayne to check how he was feeling, she moved on to nearby club China White for a serious boozing session.

There she bumped into Janet Jackson who tapped her on the shoulder and said, 'Hope your guy gets better.'

There was another infamous girls outing to Dublin, where Coleen hooked up with her pals from Croxteth to enjoy a night of partying until 5 a.m. She danced the night away at the Burlington Hotel with a gang of thirteen girlfriends, knocking back bottles of red and white wine, vodka and diet Coke. Coleen also did the now-famous comedy walk – immortalised by Peter Kay – when the band played 'Is This The Way To Amarillo?'

She chatted amiably to a constant stream of autograph hunters, wearing a stunning green dress by Italian label Missoni. Coleen also danced with former England star Paul Gascoigne and chatted to Westlife's Nicky Byrne before leaving the party in the hotel's conference room to continue revelling at Dublin's trendy Lillies' Bordello.

The inevitable shopping trip followed the next day. Accompanied by two minders and her friend Gemma, Coleen spent two hours wandering around Ireland's exclusive Brown Thomas, browsing through designer lines Chloe, Prada and Dolce & Gabbana before being ushered off to a private dressing room to try on her favourites. In true Coleen style, a pink Juicy Couture tracksuit, worth £200, was one of her purchases.

And Coleen's hangover cure for all this excess? 'Eating a McDonalds and drinking loads of water sitting on the sofa watching TV,' she says.

Coleen admits it has taken her time to grow into her new money's-no-object lifestyle. She was just a girl from the backstreets who cherished a dream and could be found peering through the windows of her favourite fashion boutiques, unable to afford the slinky items within. But, almost overnight, that all changed. Suddenly, she could afford anything that took her fancy, often buying for the sake of it – she admits she didn't always wear everything she bought.

And she was bound to make mistakes which left the fashion world sniggering at her style. She says: 'My mum and dad keep clippings from papers and sometimes I will look back on the old pictures. It's like, "What was I thinking when I wore that?" I was just sixteen when they first started taking my picture so your style naturally changes. But I don't feel pressure to dress smartly every time I go out just because people expect me to. If I wake up in the morning and run out for a newspaper I will just chuck on my tracksuit. Sometimes photographers pop up, so if they get me on a bad day that's tough. I don't mind.'

Not much upsets Coleen these days. She has a fairytale lifestyle and the common sense to recognise that it makes her a subject of fascination. Recently, she was caught in a picture with her hair curlers but there is only one thing she admits can get her goat – impolite drivers.

She said: 'I get road rage. If I let someone pull out in front of me and they don't thank me, I go mad, beeping my horn and waving. People can be so rude. That bothers me more than getting caught in my curlers. If I go to the hairdressers before a night out I will often leave the rollers in and take them out at home. I don't care what people think so long as my hair looks good when I go out.'

Inevitably, the siren of fame has drawn Wayne and Coleen inexorably closer to the high life. Like many other famous couples, they attended the Beckhams'

Full Length and Fabulous pre-World Cup party held at their mansion in Sawbridgeworth, Hertfordshire, in May 2006. It was the bash of the year and a Who's Who of top celebrities flocked to the party.

England's skipper David greeted his team-mates, led by Wayne who was then recovering from his broken foot. The Manchester United striker arrived hand in hand with Coleen, who was wearing a borrowed £200,000 necklace.

She said: 'I was so excited about the Beckhams' Full Length and Fabulous party to celebrate the World Cup. With the help of Justine at my favourite boutique Cricket, I chose a beautiful Alice Temperley dress. I try to wear English designers to show my loyalty to the country. I also wore a Temperley dress to the wedding of the Manchester United physio recently.

'Being a bit short means I have to wear some very high heels I can hardly walk in. But I don't care, even if the shoes are killing me, I won't take them off!'

The stars paid £2,000 each to attend the party at Beckingham Palace, in a marquee the size of an aircraft hangar. All money raised was donated to UNICEF and a children's charity run by the Beckhams. And despite two inches of rain, Victoria was determined the charity event would go down in history.

England heroes included Rio Ferdinand, Joe Cole,

Frank Lampard, Michael Owen and Gary Neville. While wonderkid Theo Walcott, 17, brought girlfriend Melanie Slade, also 17. Kate Moss, Elle McPherson, Ozzy Osbourne with wife Sharon and daughter Kelly and film hunk Christian Slater all delighted the crowds who thronged by the gates to see stars arrive. Actor Ray Winstone and celebrity interior designer Kelly Hoppen were also amongst the VIPs. In total, more than 350 guests mingled at the bash, whose invitations were printed on thick white card with silver letters, created by Sienna Miller's stepmum Kelly Hoppen.

Presenter Graham Norton and Radio 2 DJ Chris Evans spent hours rehearsing their scripts for the evening, making sure the celebrity guests were the butt of their jokes. Meanwhile, James Brown, godfather of soul, banged out 'Sex Machine' before a special duet with Robbie Williams, who also entertained guests with his own set. Radio One DJ Spoony, a pal of the Beckhams, and DJ Russell, a new kid on the block, took over from David – trying his hand as a DJ on the night – to spin a few discs. Fiery TV chef Gordon Ramsay did the catering and American illusionist David Blaine performed the magic.

Victoria even hired a Spanish language expert for some top tips for her speech, which she delivered in the language of her new home. After dinner, she stood up to give a special speech to say farewell to her husband and the rest of the England squad.

The theme for the extravaganza was a magical woodland since Victoria wanted to create an enchanted evening for her guests. Entertainers were dressed as fairies and the orange and lemon trees – especially flown in from Spain – twinkled with thousands of lights.

It was all kicked off with a flypast of four planes – after the Beckhams had cancelled one featuring Second World War aircraft for fear of upsetting the Germans.

After dinner Graham Norton did the auction – but was ordered to tone down his normally outrageous antics. He was in charge of the gavel as guests bid for items including a £500,000 Dubai apartment, Posh's £1 million diamond necklace, a Bentley and diamond-encrusted watches worth £60,000.

Coleen confided on the evening: 'I am dead worried for Wayne because he had that foot injury but I am sure he will be brilliant. I am hoping to take a friend with me to the World Cup because I will hardly get to see him. So I will spend a lot of time with the other girls. Luckily we all get on dead well, so it should be a lot of fun – although we'll be dead nervous for the men, too.'

But despite the bling, bling lifestyle and invite to the smartest showbiz do of the year, both Wayne and Coleen remain sure of their roots.

Said Coleen: 'I do get invited to some wonderful places and mingle with famous people but at the end of the day, when me and Wayne go home, it's just us, the way we always are. It's lovely to have the chance to dress up and go to posh places but there's nothing like coming home and remembering who you are and why you were there. That's not real life – what happens at home is where it is real.'

Coleen is keen to stress that they are like any other normal couple. She cooks – usually pasta, fish, rice. Or if it's a takeaway they have Chinese. If Wayne hasn't got a match on they will have a bottle of white wine. On a Sunday Coleen washes their clothes while Wayne has a lie in or she does the tidying up while he plays on the Playstation. A scene played out at thousands of homes across the land.

'Neither me nor Coleen are very domesticated,' explains Wayne. 'Coleen does the washing and her mum comes round and irons and hoovers. If I leave anything on the floor Coleen goes mad, but then, when she is going out with the girls, she goes out in one outfit and leaves about 50 on the floor. We do argue about that, just silly things like that.

'We still go to Coleen's mum's for dinner a couple

of times a week and she does a great spaghetti Bolognese or fish because she knows I like it. We visit my mum and dad or aunts and cousins every week too. We are normal people who enjoy doing normal things. We like a glass of wine, watching TV and being together. Our ideal night is at a family party or going for dinner.'

They do like going out to fancy restaurants, on occasion too, but they are not worried about being seen in some less than trendy eating establishments. 'We still like going down the chippie sometimes to get our dinner' says Coleen. When they do go out Wayne always chooses a chicken Caesar salad – and the couple's favourite is Wing's Chinese in Manchester. Coleen loves their chicken in black bean sauce and Singapore vermicelli. 'I have to admit I love Italian and Chinese food, but we're not into Indian. Crisps are my big downfall.'

However, nothing beats her mum's Sunday roast. 'I did a spaghetti Bolognese recently and it was quite good. I have a go at cooking and, as I get older, I think I'll get better but we still often pop round to my mum's on a Sunday. It's a family day for me and Wayne. We always go for a roast and watch the *EastEnders* omnibus.

'I love spending weekends with my family but if I had to choose someone else, I would love to spend a weekend with the Osbourne family because they seem so hilarious and I bet they have a lot of fun.'

Another example of how the couple have stayed true to their roots lies in the fact that they are still close to their childhood friends and prefer their company to that of other celebrities.

'Two of my best mates are Bradley and John who I have known since primary school,' explains Wayne. 'They come round to our house a couple of times a week and stay over. We get a DVD, a glass of wine, Italian takeaway and just sit around and chat.

'It is really funny because Bradley, who is a printer, is an Everton fan and John, who is a builder, is a Liverpool fan. They sit and argue about the football teams but I am not allowed to join in. If I try to say anything they say, "Shut up, what do you know anyway." We never discuss football, I can't get a word in edgeways. They help keep me grounded... it would be impossible to be big headed around them. They treat me the same as they did when we were kids.'

Coleen admits that a normal day in the Rooney household is much duller than most would imagine. She told *New Woman*: 'We don't have any staff do anything for us, we do the same things as millions of other people every day – the washing, the cleaning. I still make mistakes and mix the colours in the washing machine so the whites come out grey but I'm getting better at it. There's no way we would have staff, that's just not me.'

So, while the couple enjoy all the trappings of wealth, they still hanker after the simple life. They often shun fancy restaurants to enjoy two-meals-for-a-fiver at their local pub, The Bollin Fee in Wilmslow, Greater Manchester, where they have become such regulars, nobody blinks an eyelid when they walk in.

The pub's manager Aaron Fraser reckons the couple enjoy his pub because they never get mobbed. He says: 'We don't treat footballers any differently from any other customers and they are always welcome here. Wayne especially likes the fact that you can get plain and simple English food and it's served quickly.'

And says Coleen: 'Everyone thinks Wayne is this big fat person who scoffs hamburgers all the time but it isn't true. It really annoys me. It does my head in that people believe that.'

While Coleen and Wayne could easily vanish into the word of celebrity, it says much for them both that they remain close to their families and staunchly loyal to their old mates. Both still visit the downtrodden streets of Croxteth where they are received without a second glance thanks to the fact that they have remained determined to stay close to their roots.

Both obviously enjoy the benefits money can bring but neither are awed or owned by it. As two young people with the world at their feet it is a tribute to them that they remain true to themselves.

CHAPTER SEVEN

coleen's goals

AS recently as 2005, Coleen was a girl who could do nothing right. Critics dubbed her a shopaholic whose only talent was pounding the streets of Liverpool – spend, spend, spending fiancé Wayne's £50,000 a month salary. She was damned for everything, from the way she dressed to her weight and even the way she spoke.

Still only twenty years old, Coleen was devastated by the criticisms. But she has come out laughing.

There's no denying that Coleen likes to shop, spending up to £10,000 in a single spree and even admitting that she often never wears some of the clothes that she buys. For instance, she has more than £30,000 worth of handbags in her wardrobe –

and haute couture outfits running past the £200,000 mark. Add to that shoes – and she does – and accessories and it's not surprising that Coleen earned the wrath of critics, especially for her bling, bling fashion style.

But today Coleen has, with the help of a personal trainer and stylists, turned herself into a groomed beauty. In fact, it was Coleen who stole the show when she joined Charles and Camilla at the *Chronicles of Narnia* world premiere in a dazzling white Prada dress, set off by a Chloé handbag, in December 2005.

And it is Coleen who has replaced Victoria Beckham in the fashion stakes, recently voted as the girl most others would like to look like in a LG mobile phone poll. The fashion world has taken note. And so have the critics.

But Coleen, a bright girl, isn't about to forget the sniping. She is proud of what she has achieved, slimming down to a curvy size 10 – but there's a lot more to Coleen than a mere dress size. She is determined to carve a career in her own right, inflamed by claims that she is a gold-digger who hangs on to Wayne for dear life because she is in love with the lifestyle his money can buy.

And to prove it, she has earned a whopping £5.5 million of her own money since 2005 starting with the *Vogue* photo shoot which helped launch her as an attractive proposition to a surprised media. Business experts insist that will double by the end of the 2006. 'I want to be a person in my own right,' she says, 'not just somebody who is well known for hanging off the arm of a footballer or like a Stepford Wife.' And she's going the right way about it.

Coleen has always been driven and ambitious, a fact that was largely ignored by critics who seemed to want to damn her if she did and damn her if she didn't. The lass was so upset by the labels thrust on her by the media, that she was determined to try and prove she was not the airhead she had been made out to be. Her first step towards this was agreeing to a Channel Five documentary called *Coleen's Secrets* in 2005. 'I wanted people to see me for who I really am,' explained Coleen, 'not the way I was being portrayed and tagged.'

But the choice was unwise. It was Coleen's first foray into TV – a medium she would like to work more at – but it served only to reinforce her image as a shopaholic, concentrating, as it did, on her efforts to find a suitable outfit for a posh function.

Still, Coleen was determined to rise to the challenge of making her way to her own bank account. Today, she has one at Coutts & Co. Not bad for a girl who was hanging out in a puffa jacket outside the chippie on a Croxteth council estate three years ago.

Coleen has been portrayed as an airhead who fell on her feet when she met Wayne, squandering his cash on wardrobes full of designer clothes. She's also been criticised for never having done a day's work in her life.

But it was only in 2002 that she was working as a sales assistant in New Look. She worked on Saturdays, and in the weeks leading up to Christmas, she did a few nights after school as well. Coleen thought it was great because she got 50 per cent off – but of course her wages were gone on the first day.

She'd just started going out with Wayne at the time, and it was coming up to his birthday and Christmas, so she got the job in order to save up some money to buy him some presents. She bought him a jumper and some cordless earphones for his birthday, and a ring for Christmas.

Being able to afford presents for Wayne wasn't the only perk on the job. After work, the shop assistants were allowed to try on new stock.

In answer to her critics Coleen said: 'I've never been work shy. I used to be a cleaner too. My auntie used to clean chalets at Pontin's and I went with her. So I'm a lucky girl for what I have now but I don't take anything for granted.

'I enjoy working,' she says. 'I am dedicated and I would hate to be just sitting around the house waiting for Wayne to come home. I would be bored silly. He trains very hard, he is away most of the day and has always been worried that I would be lonely. He is glad for me to work, he is proud of me and it means I can buy him little gifts out of my own money. It doesn't feel the same if I do it by spending his money.'

Countless fashion shoots followed on from the *Vogue* spectacular, including *Hello!*, *CosmoGirl*, *You*, *Closer* and *More* magazines. But this time, Coleen got paid – her agent Paul Stretford, who also handles Wayne, made sure of that.

Says Coleen: 'The first thing I bought with my first pay cheque was a £2,000 Fendi bag. It felt good to be able to do that. I thought, "I've worked hard for that money, I deserve to treat myself".'

And her new-found independent wealth meant she was also able to splash out £700,000 on a new home for her family in Liverpool's exclusive Sandfield Park – and, in June 2006, £177,000 of her own cash on a silver Aston Martin Vanquish for Wayne as a good luck present for the World Cup.

Wayne – still recovering from a broken metatarsal in his foot prior to the 2006 World Cup tournament – was delighted with the 200 mph supercar as he arrived at Coleen's parents' home to find it waiting outside. It was just the tonic to cheer him up as he anxiously waited to see if he was fit enough to play in the tournament. And after completing a promising World Cup training session, Wayne put the Aston through its paces on his way home, grinning from ear to ear.

He already has a string of luxury cars, including a BMW X5, Cadillac Escalade and Mercedes CLK – and in 2005 he bought Coleen a £60,000 Mercedes AMG55 after he splashed out on another Mercedes SLK 200, worth over £29,000. But the Aston gift has become a firm favourite.

Coleen's childhood ambition was to become an actress – and it is still a strong-held desire. The acting had been a dream since she started drama and dancing classes at the age of seven, 'but I've always had in my mind that it's a hard thing to get into. But then look at Wayne – you never know what's round the corner.'

She also did some work experience on a local magazine and fantasised about having her own fashion column. 'I wanted to get out and go places – that is what I would have liked to do.'

However, much had changed since her early aspirations when still a young girl. Her first ambition in life was to work in the sweet shop next to her house and, then, she wanted to be a teacher – but everyone wants to be a teacher at some point. Then she wanted to do something with drama, then journalism, before going back to drama again.

'I was always involved in productions at school' she said. 'I was never the lead because it was all musicals and I can't sing, so I'd just get the next part, but I was always a man. Because it was an all girls' school, we had to play the lads' roles as well. We did *Bugsy Malone* and I was Fat Sam. Wayne used to come and watch – he took the whole cast out for dinner one night, I was really made up. He's lovely and thoughtful like that.'

Since first gaining fame as Wayne's other half, she has enjoyed a fleeting appearance in *Hollyoaks* and has said she would love to appear in *Coronation Street*. But she wants to do it on her own merit, not just because she has a famous boyfriend, and to that end she is taking acting and elocution lessons to soften her Scouse accent.

Says Coleen: 'I want my own identity. I love the idea of being in *Coronation Street*. When I saw Kym Marsh in the show I thought, "Great, that is the kind of role I could pull off".'

But first, Coleen is determined to earn her way to an acting career. She plans to join a local drama group before deciding on whether to take a professional performing arts course. 'I have been offered a lot of roles but I have turned them down because the timing isn't right.'

One such role was an invitation from Louis Walsh for her to appear on *Celebrity X Factor*. Coleen admits: 'I met Louis at the Beckhams' World Cup party. I found myself dancing with the Osbournes on one side and P Diddy on the other. It was mad! During dinner I sat beside Cheryl Tweedy, which was great because I've known her for a while. Louis Walsh came over and asked me to go on *Celebrity X Factor*. Cheryl was saying, "Go on, give it a go". But I was adamant. I can't sing to save my life – I won't even go on a karaoke. I used to be in the school choir but I couldn't sing. It was just so I could get into productions. There's no way I would have done it but I was flattered to be asked.'

Coleen is cautious of drawing more criticism and, with that in mind, is set on becoming a celebrity in her own right. She recognises that her fame is reflected from Wayne, the biggest soccer star since George Best, and she has a lot to live up to. She doesn't want to compete with Wayne, but she wants him to win by having a loving girlfriend who can stand on her own two feet, and by his side, without being clingy.

It is healthy for Coleen to work, giving the couple

another shared interest. Wayne cannot be the be all and end all of her world. The responsibility is too great and, anyway, she needs to fill her own time to shore up her self respect and esteem.

That's not to say she doesn't give 100 per cent to the relationship. What it means is Wayne is free to focus on his soccer without worrying whether she is occupied or unhappy.

She told me: 'I want to be able to hold my own in the acting world and I won't really be able to do that without a proper grounding. That means drama school. My big dream is to follow Jennifer Ellison or Billie Piper – I am a big fan of them both.

'My dream role would be the part of Mickey's girlfriend in Willy Russell's Merseyside set musical *Blood Brothers*. I studied the play at school and have seen it loads of times. Joining a local drama group will be a great way of learning and a good way to meet new people. Eventually I would love to be in a two-part drama like the ones Tamzin Outhwaite does.'

But before Coleen embarks on the serious business of learning to act she dipped her toe in the water with a fitness DVD.

The proposition of an exercise DVD followed a holiday in 2005 with Wayne to Barbados. She was photographed poolside in her bikini, and the producers at Universal Pictures spotted her potential.

She says: 'I had been going to the gym and it wasn't like I had lost loads of weight but by body shape was different. I got approached to do the fitness DVD a year previously but turned it down because I didn't have a reason – you can't just do one if you've not changed or become fitter. Then I was asked again. I'd been working out and lost a few pounds so I thought, "Well, now is my chance so I agree." I am glad because I really enjoyed doing it.'

Universal hooked her up with a personal trainer – and she pocketed £150,000 to reveal her exercise secrets. 'Making the video was hard work,' she explained. 'People think you just do one thing and the video is done in a day. I was getting tired and we had to repeat the exercises. I was done in for a week after but I was really toned up.

'I do loads of squats and lunges which is the best thing to do to tone up your bum. I have relished doing all the work. It was exciting and it has been good for me.'

Next in Coleen's move towards independence were sponsorship deals with the likes of Nike, LG phones and Asda, and a two-book deal with HarperCollins, one to reveal her beauty and lifestyle tips and the second a novel, all amounting to a cool £5 million in her bank account.

Coleen, who helped design her own range of

clothing for Asda, is now the face of trendy LG's Chocolate phone. Launched in Europe in May 2006, the sleek phone gained international credibility due to the fact that its glossy bones resemble a block of the finest chocolate. Owners include Brit babe Kelly Brook and her fiancé Billy Zane, actress Gwyneth Paltrow, former 007 Pierce Brosnan, heart-throb Jude Law and Coldplay singer Chris Martin.

Coleen donned a black pencil skirt, smart white shirt, black stilettos and a pair of prim glasses to promote the phone handset – on the day she and Wayne were voted the celebrity couple most theatre-goers would like to see on the West End stage.

They beat off stiff competition from A-list celebs including David and Victoria Beckham, to be crowned the most favoured couple to tread the boards. *Celebrity Big Brother* winner Chantelle and her Ordinary Boys fiancé Preston came in a close second, followed by Jordan and husband Peter André.

At the phone launch Coleen said: 'To me style is about being true to yourself while at the same time using fashion to make a statement. Having the LG Chocolate phone in my hand does that perfectly – and it works as an accessory for any outfit. It is unique, sleek and exactly the right size to pop into my handbag for any occasion. I liked it, that's why I agreed to promote it.'

An LG spokeswoman cooed: 'Coleen was a natural choice for the launch of the LG Chocolate phone. She is stylish, everyone can identify with her and, like the phone, she is irresistible.'

Wayne already has a £3 million deal with Nike but they were quick to snap up Coleen to Nike Women Sportwear once she had proved that she was a gym devotee enjoying her new slimline figure. She will promote her own line of sportswear called Nike C and model a range of tracksuits and leotards all carrying the C – for Coleen, naturally – logo and a far cry from the Juicy Couture she favoured.

Supermarket giant Asda came next, with a £1.5 million deal for Coleen to spearhead a new summer fashion range. The range, called Must Have, is the latest from its George brand and Coleen has already been seen out and about in a stone-coloured summer dress from the collection. The new Asda collection features up-to-the-minute fashion items which speed from the catwalk into stores and change on a monthly basis.

Angela Spindler, global marketing director for George, said: 'We are delighted to have Coleen on board. She epitomises the young, vibrant woman we are targeting and is always ahead of the style stakes.'

Coleen added: 'I am really excited about it. Everyone knows how much I love fashion and at these prices I can buy the whole range for £250.'

Another string to Coleen's bow is journalism – she also writes a column for *Closer* magazine. 'Wayne watches football while I write it on a Sunday,' she says.

It is self-evident that the fact that Coleen has a column in one of the biggest selling magazines means she is a popular figure with young women who lap up her chatty style and the titbits about her life with Wayne, fashion likes and dislikes and general gossip about herself.

All these endorsements were all very well, but it was not until Coleen appeared on the hard-hitting telly programme *Tonight With Trevor McDonald*, presenting her feature on the funding of hospices, that the critics were silenced.

The show, which reduced Coleen to tears, dealt with her own sister Rosie's degenerative disability Rett syndrome and cast Coleen in a whole new light. It was her first foray into presenting herself as a serious role model, rather than the vacant airhead she has been portrayed as – and it earned her plaudits all round.

For the first time, the real Coleen emerged, compassionate, kind, deeply caring and gentle. The idea that she was one dimensional and her only talent was for shopping was dispelled instantly by the moving documentary and the honest emotion she allowed viewers to see.

She said: 'I was flattered to be asked to do the *Tonight...* show and felt it was a worthy cause, particularly in the light of my sister's own disability.'

The *Mirror*'s Sue Carroll said: 'To change the way one is perceived normally requires expensive public relations and what is now called rebranding. Coleen achieved it when she presented *Tonight With Trevor McDonald* on children's hospices. It worked partly because her sister Rosie, who suffers from Rett syndrome, stays in a hospice two days a month. But mainly it was due to something that can't be manufactured – Coleen's compassion and conviction that these places are outrageously underfunded by the government.

'I trust her shopaholic airhead tag has been banished forever.'

And the *Daily Telegraph*'s Alice Thompson agreed: 'Congratulations Coleen. Wayne had it easy – he had a natural talent for football. Coleen had no such asset. Yet without having any of the same raw ability, she has managed to eclipse her fiancé off the field. She is not particularly academic or beautiful, but she works hard while continuing to be extremely loyal to her man. She may not have achieved anything amazing but she is unfailingly kind and polite. Best of all, she never whinges. She appreciates her luck and makes the most of it.'

Coleen agreed to host the documentary because the cause was close to her heart. As it was her first TV presenting job she was naturally nervous, so Sir Trevor himself gave her professional tips on how best to perform.

Said Coleen: 'I had lunch with Sir Trevor and he gave me loads of useful tips so it was great, he was so supportive. It was really hard to film as the subject matter was so upsetting. But it is something I care deeply about and the end result was more than worth it.'

Coleen worked hard while filming the moving documentary and impressed with her professional approach. Over the course of three months she travelled to hospices around the country. She went to Claire House, where her disabled sister Rosie is cared for, and to Francis House in Manchester where little Kirsty Howard – who has caught so many people's attention – is cared for, as well as the East Anglia children's hospice in Cambridge.

She spoke to families who had children in hospices and families who had lost children and continue to get support and comfort from the hospice carers, as well as chief executives and fundraisers.

As she explains: 'I learned much that touched me and some things that shocked me. Britain's hospices receive, on average, between two and five per cent of their income from the government. Adult hospices get closer to 40 per cent. It costs up to £4 million to set up a hospice and about £1.5 million a year to run it. Of course, there are a lot of voluntary workers in hospices.

'At Claire House many of the people who cook and clean for the children and their families are volunteers. But medical staff have to be paid and equipment needs to be bought. We recently had to buy a wheelchair for Rosie and it is unbelievable how expensive they are. I am in a very lucky position financially but I do know that a lot of people are not.

'Hospices rely on fundraising events to keep going. I went to a fashion show in Selfridges in Manchester in aid of Francis House. It was a glamorous night. There was champagne and the girls from *Hollyoaks* and *Coronation Street* were modelling – I bought a pair of shoes.

'But after working on the *Tonight* show I couldn't help wonder whether hospices should have to put on events such as that just to keep going.

'A lot of people I spoke to on the night assumed that hospices were part of the NHS. But they are not and some are struggling to survive. At East Anglia staff were worried that they may have to start reducing the care they offer because the National

Lottery funding they received the year previously had run out.

'Its fantastic facilities are going to waste because the hospice is having to reduce the number of days it is open during the week and limit the number of families who receive respite care.'

Clearly passionate about this subject, it was the story of cancer victim Shadia Mathers, a 15-year-old girl facing death, which moved Coleen to tears. 'She was only fifteen but she was diagnosed with cancer,' explained Coleen. 'It started in her leg but chemotherapy didn't work and it spread until the doctor had to tell her there was nothing more they could do.

'Her mum Debbie told me how Shadia had asked, "Will I reach my 17th birthday?' The doctor said no. Shadia said, "Will I reach my 16th birthday?" The doctor said he couldn't tell her. Sometimes when people are faced with the worst possible news they find strength they didn't know they had. Shadia told the doctor there and then that she would reach her 18th birthday.'

Debbie recounted how, as Shadia became more and more unwell, it was suggested that she should go into Francis House for respite care but she rejected the idea. Shadia thought she would be surrounded by dying people and that it would be a terrible place to visit because of that.

So at first the staff from Francis House visited the family at home. They took Shadia shopping when she wasn't strong enough to walk. They made sandwiches for her little sisters' packed lunches and took them to school when Shadia was so ill her mum was scared to leave her side. Eventually Shadia agreed to look at Francis House and was amazed at what she found, as Coleen explains.

'Her mum and dad Richard had planned her 18th party at a local pub but she was too ill to go. They assumed they would have to cancel but Francis House held the party for her there instead. They put up a sign saying, 'Welcome to the Lea Arms' and brought in everybody who would have been at the pub to celebrate. It probably sounds strange to some people to celebrate anything in a hospice but it meant the world to Shadia and her family.'

Tragically, she died about two weeks later.

The day Coleen spent with Shadia's family touched her deeply, perhaps because Shadia and her were of a similar age. Coleen went home that night and just started crying. She said: 'Wayne asked me what was wrong and all I could think about was how lucky we are and how much we take for granted.

'Shadia's dad still goes for counselling at Francis House. She had three little sisters and they go there to talk to children their own age who have brothers or sisters who are dying or have passed away.

'Debbie couldn't go back to the hospice herself at the time, it was too upsetting for her because it was so associated with Shadia's last days, but the counsellor visited her at home.

'In some cases, a hospice is a bereaved family's only real support. I know how much a children's hospice means to the families of children who are suffering from a life limiting illness. And I know that their work carries on after the death of the child. Now I have learned how hard it is for some of these hospices to keep going and I feel passionately that it is vital that they do.

'Wayne and I do what we can but children's hospices should receive enough money each year to know that they are secure on a basic level. They could still raise funds but they could be confident that they would not have to close their doors to sick children and their families because the cash was running out.

'My sister Rosie, who is eight now, has brought so much joy to our family. Of course, we wish she could be healthy but for her sake, not our own, because mum and dad and me and my brothers have never felt that her care was a burden.

'A situation like ours could happen to any family.

But whatever life a sick child has left should be as fulfilling as possible – and that is what hospices are all about. They make a child's life the easiest and most delightful journey it can possibly be. That is really worth spending money on.

'People see me as Wayne Rooney's girlfriend or a shopaholic but I am just a normal girl who loves my family life and my sister. I still try to see her most days. You never know what she wants or you never know what is wrong with her because she can't tell you. That is grounding.'

Being a subject so close to her own heart, Coleen was moved to criticise the government for their perceived lack of funding for hospices. Clearly, the good that they do and the happiness that they spread among patients, often in their last months of life, is undeniable.

'What makes me really angry,' she explains, 'and what I just don't understand is why children's hospices like Claire House receive hardly a penny from government. Instead they rely almost entirely on charitable donations to fund the amazing work they do. I found the whole thing very emotional. Hospices are places of laughter and love. The children get that little bit more attention which makes them feel special. I am no politician but it is obvious hospice funding is a real problem in this country.'

Generous Wayne is a secret donor to several charities and Coleen is doing her bit too, organising a star-studded polo match in 2007 to raise cash for the Rett Syndrome Association UK.

But there's one person who already believe Coleen has done more than many in her position – Shadia's mum.

Debbie told *Closer* magazine: 'Meeting Coleen was part of my grieving process. She is so down to earth and much more than just a footballers' wife. It meant so much to me that she cried for my girl. Anything Coleen does to highlight the amazing work they do can only be good news. Shadia would have loved someone so famous visiting her home. I am sure she is looking down from heaven and smiling because of it.'

The best news is that the government have since pledged an extra £27 million to help children's hospices. In response Coleen said: 'I feel very passionately about helping hospices. Many are struggling with resources – I am so happy with the government's pledge. I had a lot of feedback from the programme. Lots of people said it really opened their eyes to the problem and hospices have received many more donations because of it. I'm so glad it made a difference.'

And ITV bosses were said to be so impressed with Coleen's one-off special, commitment and professionalism, they have decided to sign her up on a two-year contract.

Coleen, who has also opened a PR firm with her mum Colette, Speed 9849 Ltd, says: 'I haven't got a clue what I will be doing in five years time. I take each day as it comes. But I enjoyed presenting the documentary and hope I get the chance to do some more TV work.'

That seems more than likely. Just a few weeks after making a success of the documentary, Coleen topped an Internet poll of 'Women to Watch in 2006', beating actresses Sienna Miller and Keira Knightley. And, inevitably, she also overtook Sienna to win the title of Celebrity Shopper of the Year!

'It had been a long time to get to where I am now,' says Coleen. 'I had offers from the start but I have waited for the rights one to come along. I have always been keen. Even at school I was hard working. It is a Catholic thing, my parents drilled it into me to work hard.

'I think I have always wanted to be where I am now. I like having my own column and it was an honour to work with Sir Trevor. Hopefully I will get further offers. At school I was always interested in doing media studies, English literature and performing arts – I am passionate about becoming an actress.

'Wayne is dead chuffed for me. But I wouldn't say I have changed much. My personal life is still very much the same. My lifestyle has certainly changed, but not me. I can do a lot more things now, things you dream of as a kid.

'People think it is all glamorous but it is not all of the time. Yeah, I get invited to fancy premieres and stuff which is dead nice. But I think that is the only thing that has changed. I still have days doing stuff like I have always done, like grocery shopping and putting it all away when I get home. The only thing I want is to come across as myself. For who I am. For going out and having a go.'

And on current form, it seems Coleen's going the right way about it.

CHAPTER EIGHT

rivals to the throne

PRESS interest in the real-life footballers' wives has flourished since the start of the fictional ITV drama of the same name, but this attention really escalated during the 2006 World Cup in Germany.

The wives and girlfriends (or WAGS as they were famously dubbed) all stayed together in a five-star hotel in Baden-Baden and garnered as many, if not more, column inches for their drinking and shopping exploits, than their men did on the pitch. And predictably Coleen, fiancée of one of world football's brightest stars and a celebrity in her own right, generated as much interest as anyone else.

But in the race for top WAG, who are her rivals and who might she have to watch out for in the future if she is to maintain her position as Queen of the Tabloids?

If Victoria Beckham is considered Queen Bee as the ultimate footballers' wife, she has already felt the sting of rivals clamouring to fill her shoes. While Posh – a super skinny size six – is falling out of fashion, Coleen has stolen her crown. Coleen, a toned size 10, looks a glowing picture of health.

While Posh forged a career in girl power, Coleen's charm lies in her down-to-earth appeal and vulnerability. For a generation of adolescents who want to be famous for being famous, she is the poster girl of the celebrity set and whatever High Street fashion Coleen wears now launches a selling frenzy, just like Posh in the past. In fact, Coleen's selling power is now so great that she has received a flurry of requests from designers begging her to help promote their creations ahead of the Christmas party season in 2006.

Victoria Beckham used to be the most talked about woman in Britain. Her clothes, her love life, her kids – the media couldn't get enough of her. But now there's a new girl in town – Coleen – who has stealthily stolen the limelight from under Victoria's nose.

Wayne and Coleen even favour the same posh Manchester hotel as the Beckhams – Salford's Lowry, an elegant, understated hotel where the presidential suite they prefer costs £1,500 a night and boasts a baby grand piano, its own kitchen, massive marble bathroom and great views.

Wise management and a clever PR campaign have seen Coleen re-positioned in the market, from the tabloid invention of airhead chav and freeloader to glossy champion of children's hospices who works for her own living. In 2006 alone, Coleen earned almost as much as her footballing fiancé, and the duo are fast becoming a power couple, like the Beckhams before them.

However, Coleen's still the kind of girl who will pop out for a pint of milk in her slippers. It has endeared her to her generation as well as the media, for her modesty, lack of prima donna behaviour and professional approach; she always turns up on time, a rare quality and courtesy amongst celebrities.

But Coleen's not the only soccer princess waiting to fill Victoria's four-inch stilettos. Alex Curran, the fiancée of Liverpool and England star Steven Gerrard, is also a glamorous shop 'til you drop merchant, spending Gerrard's £55,000 a week fortune at the same rate as Coleen – and in the same shops. But Alex is riled by suggestions that she copies Coleen's style, despite the fact that they are often pictured separately wearing the same expensive outfit.

Says Alex: 'Coleen and I dress alike because we are from the same area and around the same age with similar lives. We are bound to go to the same shops and even occasionally end up wearing the same things. I wear designer clothes but I also wear High Street stuff too. Sometimes you can't beat a top from H&M or Top Shop. I think Coleen dresses well for her age. She always looks smart but she is a bit more conservative than me. I am more daring.'

And, she told the *Sunday Mirror*, her life is nothing like that of the footballers' wives on the telly. 'It is not all celebrity parties and trendy clubs. I spend my days looking after our daughter Lilly Ella, two, and tidying the house, cooking and ironing. People expect me to have an army of helpers but it is just me – although my mum and Steven's mum are a massive support.'

Alex, a former manicurist from the rough Norris Green area of Liverpool insists she is no fashion victim. She said: 'I am up at 7 a.m. every day. I get breakfast ready, take Lilly to nursery and stop at the shops to buy something for tea. I'm not any stereotypical footballer's wife. If I see something I like at Tesco I will buy it. I am not a label snob.'

However, she does have one thing in common with her fictional namesakes – she can certainly shop. 'I know I am very lucky but sometimes I get serious guilt pangs about how much I have spent. I don't know exactly how many handbags I have but it is enough to fill a big shelf in my wardrobe. I feel bad about having so many and often end up giving them away to friends and family. I haven't counted how many pairs of shoes I own either, I definitely have more than 50 pairs.'

Alex is attempting to carve out a celebrity career of her own. Upset by sneers that she was a chav, she hired a stylist and hopes to present her own fashion show on Sky TV.

Even so, Alex still turned up wearing exactly the same outfit as Coleen – gold top, jeans and diamond jewellery – when they arrived at their German hotel, where they stayed for the 2006 World Cup, in a 60ft luxury coach with enough luggage to last most a lifetime. And just like Coleen, she flew in her own specialist tan therapist at the cost of £15,000.

Not that the girls needed to worry – each had planned a minimum of five changes of outfit a day and Victoria even packed 60 pairs of sunglasses and 30 pairs of her designer jeans in three separate sizes. And, to keep the girls occupied, the Baden-Baden hotel boasted a mind-boggling array of beauty treatments, including specialist massages, facials, body wraps and nail extensions as well as exclusive designer shops.

The World Cup saw the arrival of a new rival in town – Melanie Slade, perhaps Posh's greatest threat as a fresh-faced, seventeen year old blonde and girlfriend of England and Arsenal wunderkid Theo Walcott. She became an overnight sensation when her boyfriend was plucked from obscurity to join the England squad in Germany.

But she's not a girl from the back streets. Her dad John runs a PR firm, is vice chancellor of the local council and Mayor of Southampton. The south coast city is where Melanie still lives, working part-time in a jewellery store.

Her ex-boyfriend, Brighton & Hove Albion soccer star Ashley Jarvis, insists she has the qualities and resilience to become the ultimate footballer's wife, knocking Victoria or Coleen into a cocked hat.

'I definitely think she's got what it takes to become the next Posh or overtake Coleen,' he says. 'She's a bit of a shopaholic, very image conscious. She spends a lot of time doing her make-up and using sunbeds to top up her tan. She even tried to get me to go with her but I refused! She loved watching *Footballers' Wives* on the telly and *Dream Team*, and she's into all designer gear. When we went on holiday to Egypt in 2005 she bought a Chanel purse, a Gucci bag and a Ted Baker bag. And her favourite colour is pink.'

Like Wayne, Theo began playing football when he was aged just seven and insists he is an ordinary boy whose favourite meal is his dad Don's shepherd's pie. He has now stolen Rooney's crown as the youngest lad to be invited to play for England and, like Wayne, has a close-knit family.

He's also unpretentious, telling how he wooed Melanie by handing her his phone number while she was standing outside the shop where she works holding a basket. His mate had spotted Mel first – and walked past, putting his phone number in the basket. Theo, blushing, handed her his number himself.

He told *The Sun*: 'I didn't hit her with any cheesy chat ups. She was really shy. She just contacted me and we've been good since. She's brilliant, she's gorgeous. We're not the type who like to party hard – we're more likely to spend time with our families. I'm just a quiet lad, me, I don't even like clubbing. I'm a family man.

'My one weakness is fashion. It's a big part of my life. I like Armani and Hugo Boss. There's no way fame will go to my head, nor Mel's. I won't let it. We have our families around us.'

Melanie showed her unmistakable star potential in her first ever photo shoot. Stunning Mel posed for snaps as a favour to her photography student sister Emma. She sat for half an hour displaying her toned figure in a shredded-ribbon top and gypsy skirt. Then sixteen, she was such a hit with A level students that she was invited back to model twenty times – and helped Emma get an A grade.

Melanie has already generated substantial press interest. She has already been offered a £1 million book deal, with an option for a second, and hundreds of thousands of pounds to tell her life story to various newspapers and magazines. Her father insisted that she would not accept any offers until after the World Cup and, as a PR man himself, is likely to represent her.

Melanie, middle-class, slim, polite and prettily blonde, is ripe for having her bones picked over by the fickle media and isn't the kind of girl you'd see gracing the cover of a lads' mag. Not for her fake tan, fake nails and fake hair extensions – she has a natural beauty which puts Posh, Coleen and Alex in the shade.

She made her first public appearance at a breast cancer charity photo call in May 2006 and said, 'I'm so shocked. I'm just trying to relax. I've got exams to finish and I'm just a normal girl. My friends have been great and aren't jealous of the attention I get. I even get photographed walking my dog Snoop. They think it is surreal.' And just like Coleen before her, Mel added: 'It has affected my exams but I am trying to keep my head down.'

Coleen the style icon – in 2006 she launched an advertising campaign for George at Asda (*above left*), presented an award at the Elle Style Awards (*above right*), launched the LG chocolate phone (*below left*), and won the Ariel Fashion Award for 'Best Dressed Female Celebrity' (*below right*).

Although she leads the lifestyle of an A-list celebrity, Coleen remains loyal to her old friends and family. Here she is pictured enjoying a day at the races with her mother, April 2006, and *below* on holiday in Cannes.

Coleen and Wayne enjoy a balmy summer night out on the tiles in Cannes.

With Wayne in Baden Baden during World Cup 2006.

Above: Outside Europa park in a photoshoot with the other WAGs.

Below left: Looking a little bit damp after being caught in one of the water rides.

Below right: Arriving back at the England WAGs' hotel after accompanying Wayne to England for his final scan.

Above left: Watching Wayne play for England in their match with Paraguay.

Above right: Attending the WAG party in a hotel in Baden Baden.

Below left: Coleen's reaction to Wayne being awarded a red card for a tackle he made in England's quarterfinal match against Portugal.

Below right: Consolatory shopping in London having returned early from the World Cup after England's disappointing exit.

Stylish as ever, Coleen donned a glam floral kaftan as she made her way to Nikki beach, an exclusive spot on the Saint Tropez shoreline, for a bit of well-earned rest and relaxation following the World Cup.

Coleen is determined to earn her own way and it seems that her persistence is paying off – her fashion career is going from strength to strength. This is the latest of her achievements – a still from a commercial filmed in Portugal for Asda's autumn clothing range.

Coleen extended the hand of friendship, telling *Closer* magazine: 'Good luck to Melanie. She's doing her AS levels. She delayed her trip to the World Cup so she could finish them. It reminds me of me three years ago, when I had to fly out later on my first trip with the footie wives because of my exams. It's good she's focusing on her studies.'

Melanie seems to have been accepted since her rapid introduction to the limelight following Theo's call up. However, the green eyes of jealousy may have started to burn around the pool in the players' training camp when she was immediately elevated to third in the list of most fanciable partners of the England heroes.

Alex and Cheryl Tweedy, partner of Ashley Cole, came second and third of those short-listed – but bottom of the pile was Victoria Beckham. Says Coleen: 'I get really upset by nasty comments about Victoria. We have girly chats and she is wonderful. I really love her. And anyone who knows her feels the same.'

And Wayne also has nothing but praise for the England captain David Beckham, whom he counts as a mentor and friend. It was a devastating blow to Wayne that Beckham gave up the captaincy of England. A tearful David, shaking with emotion, quit in the aftermath of England's penalty shoot-out exit to Portugal, saying he had lived the dream but the time was right to pass on the honour now England were entering a new era under new manager Steve McLaren.

Wayne told me: 'If I've got a role model it is David Beckham. He's a lovely man and has really supported me and I wanted him to be England skipper for years. I only met David a year before we went to Portugal in 2004 but I definitely rate him as a special guy. He's dead caring, a fantastic person, not at all the way people imagine – he's just normal, just like anybody else.'

Wayne believes Beckham is also a marvellous family man, the kind he would like to emulate when he has children of his own. He said: 'Me and Coleen spent time with him and his family in Portugal. It was just like being with any normal mum and dad mucking around with their kids. David is obviously a great dad and I remember thinking, "When I'm a dad, I hope I'm the kind of dad like him." They're a happy family, really close with their kids and, when me and Coleen have kids, we'd like to be a family like them.'

Wayne also credited Beckham with keeping up his spirits when, naturally, he feels vulnerable after not playing at his best. He said: 'Everybody can get a bit down if they think their performance isn't good enough. When that happened to me, David whispered a few words in my ear. He taught me loads, like how to cope with my life off the pitch. He was always a huge help, having a few words here and there about things.'

And it's no wonder Coleen doesn't want to be seen to be trying to rival Victoria. Beckham is just as full of praise for Wayne. 'Wayne is an amazing young lad and he performs well even under pressure,' says David. 'He takes everything in his stride. I'm sure he's been told about the attention and how to cope, but he just takes playing for England as if he is playing in the schoolyard or Sunday League football. He plays like a man but is still a boy.

'We are lucky to have a talent like him. People will be talking about him for a long time because he deserves it. He is a quiet lad but seems very level headed and on the pitch he is one of the biggest talents.'

But despite the apparent mutual admiration that exists between the Beckhams, Wayne and Coleen, the press do like to build up a rivalry. Even critics are plumping for Coleen as the most likely to topple Victoria Beckham from her throne.

Former *Marie Claire* editor Liz Jones says: 'I love everything about Coleen. Here at last is a young woman who enjoys the way she looks, proof that even someone who is relatively short and definitely curvy can look fabulous. She is a much better role model than Victoria Beckham and over the past year or so has demonstrated far more of a passion for fashion.

'I also like that she knows her own mind. Unlike Victoria, she gained ten GCSEs and was deputy head at her Catholic school, and also unlike Victoria, Coleen always pays full price for her designer goodies. Like any ordinary girl she sometimes gets it wrong – fake Muklaks and a gilet teamed with a lurid Juicy Couture tracksuit – and she has hair extensions, false French manicured nails, but she has bravely avoided the chavvy trampiness of most footballers' wives.

'You will never see her displaying public clinginess on the arm of her fiancé, mewing like a kitten, cleavage on display. She has too much class for that.'

And celebrity stylist Karen Clarkson says: 'They say that Victoria is in danger of losing her Tiffany crown to Coleen but in my opinion that happened long ago. OK, they both have soccer star partners and the large shopping allowance that comes with them but that is where the similarities end.

'While Victoria Beckham learned at an early age that if you've got it, you flaunt it, there is something charmingly modest about Coleen.

'Coleen favours intelligently chic labels such as Balenciaga, Chloe and Matthew Williamson while Victoria can't resist Dolce & Gabbana and Roberto Cavalli.'

Whatever the women might say, the fiercest World Cup battle wasn't fought on the pitch but in the wardrobes of the wives and girlfriends. Victoria Beckham brought several trunks of Roberto Cavalli and Chanel designs, complete with priceless Asprey jewellery.

But Coleen's pre-tournament training efforts made even Victoria look slack. Coleen had a certain look in mind, a cross between Audrey Hepburn, film star, and Christy Turlington, supermodel, elegant and refined with a glowing olive complexion.

Photographs were taken of every single garment she packed so her stylist back in England could consult with Coleen on what to wear and when while she was in Germany.

Meanwhile Coleen denies that Victoria is a role model for her. She says: 'I would like a little bit of what she has. I would like her clothes and I would like her look, but in some photographs she seems so unhappy. I don't see her as someone to look up to because I think everyone should be their own person. And I wouldn't want to have as much publicity as Victoria. I think it would be hard. I don't like it now when I go to the shops and people take pictures. And Victoria still gets more of that sort of thing than I do.'

The footballer's wife Coleen might consider a role model is Sheree Murphy, the former *Emmerdale* actress and mum-of-two who is married to Australia and Liverpool star Harry Kewell, and the woman she has become closest to. Coleen's own ambition is to become an actress and she enjoys Sheree's down-to-earth style.

On the eve on the World Cup Sheree told the *News of the World*: 'It is one big girlie holiday, with a bit of football thrown in! We hardly see the boys because we're in separate hotels but we keep busy. I look forward to nights on the town with the girls. I even take my mum out with me so she can babysit. We all know how to have fun. We've been known to go out for lunch, then carry on through the day and go out clubbing that night.'

The 'girls' are her pals Alex, Michael Owen's wife Louise and Coleen. The girls inevitably hit the headlines for their boozy nights out and shopping sprees while in Germany, filling in time until they had a chance to see their partners.

Of Coleen Sheree says, 'She is so sweet. I was out shopping with her and Alex and there was a wall of photographers waiting for her. But she never moaned, and still doesn't, even when she's not looking her best.'

Coleen, dressed in jeans and a simple white top,

certainly looked her best when she led the England wives and partners on a night out to celebrate England's victory over Paraguay on 10 June 2006. Coleen, Alex and Melanie danced on the tables of a packed bar until 4 a.m. They were joined in the frolics by Peter Crouch's girl Abigail Clancy and Elen Rives, Frank Lampard's girlfriend.

In total around ten England girls plus pals flocked to the Garibaldi Bar in Baden- Baden. Coleen's mum Colette, joined in the fun, bopping the night away on a table. According to reports, the girls enjoyed belting out a string of Barry White songs and, as Sheree predicted, got through seven bottles of champagne, twelve beers, nine vodka red bulls, fourteen vodka and lemonades, four sambucca shots, one Bacardi and coke and five liqueurs. The bar bill came to a whopping £550. And that was just for starters! The girls eventually tottered back to the £1,000 a night Brenners Park Hotel singing 'Football's Coming Home' amid gales of laughter.

The only wife not present was Victoria Beckham, who stayed in the hotel with her sons Brooklyn, Romeo and Cruz.

And if the girls weren't out partying, then they were shopping. On one occasion they hit the town for a £5,000 one-hour whirlwind spending spree. Coleen snapped up two pairs of Gucci and Dior shoes and two Dolce & Gabbana blouses for £900 – all in an impressive ten minutes! She said, somewhat understatedly: 'I just wanted to come out for a walk and I bought some bits and pieces.'

Others in the posse included Elen Rives, Joe Cole's girlfriend Carly Zucker and Wayne Bridge's other half Vanessa Perroncel. They were joined by Michael Carrick's girl Lisa Roughead and winger Stewart Downing's partner Michaela Henderson-Thynne.

Their £5,000 spree started at the Albert sunglasses shop where they bought several pairs of designer shades. Fred Lunettes and Gucci specs were favourites at £500 a pair. With a quick twist and turn they slipped next door to Monica Scholz and spent fifteen minutes choosing Gucci, D Squared, Prada, Dolce & Gabbana shoes and tops. Next stop was the Gero Mure fashion store before they hit jewellers Bijou Brigitte, picking up bracelets, earrings and rings.

Exhausted after the shopping spree the girls headed back to the hotel for an afternoon lazing by the pool – and enjoying the exotic treatments on offer. The five-star haven boasts single whirlpools, a Japanese blossom Finnish sauna, aromatherapy, hydrotherapy and Bulgari and Kanebo beauty and body spa treatments.

Just the job before several of the girls, including

Coleen and Cheryl Tweedy, joined up for a swish dinner at the town's Medici restaurant.

These days, it's hard to imagine Coleen looking anything but good when she turns on the style, with her newly-honed figure, glossy hair and glowing skin. She might not see Posh as a role model but there's no doubt she wants to fill her shoes – she'd even planned a World Cup homecoming party, just like the good luck party Posh threw to see the squad on their way.

Coleen was so impressed by the cash raised for charity at Victoria's event, she planned to host a £750,000 party in a marquee at the couple's new home in Prestbury, Cheshire. The lavish party, in aid of Claire's House Children's Hospice, where Rosie goes for respite care, was designed as a fantasy land. Bouncy castles, ice statues, men on stilts, face painters, trampolines, magicians and puppets were all planned for the event.

The couple's celebrity pals – including Victoria – all agreed to be at the party, along with Rosie and other children from the hospice. And Victoria even offered help and advice with the organisation.

From the chip shop in Croxteth to the swankiest hotel in town, Coleen has made the transition with aplomb and her star shines brightly in the firmament as she evolves into her new position as a role model, who's surely strong enough to see off her many rivals in the WAG stakes.

CHAPTER NINE
brand roo

THERE'S no doubt that Coleen's star is currently firmly hitched to that of Wayne when it comes to earning potential. Collectively, they can become a brand in the way that David and Victoria Beckham have but as things stand any injury to him is also an injury to her – without interest in Wayne, the megabucks deals would probably dry up for Coleen.

That is why it is imperative that she should carve her own 'proper' career by studying at drama school and creating her own identity, as she says she wishes to do. It will give her a string to her bow which is independent of Wayne and which will also earn her respect in her own right, helping her forge an identity which is not dependent on her fiancé's behaviour.

Even Cheryl Tweedy, Ashley Cole's fiancée, returned from the World Cup scoffing at the vanity of the WAGS. The Girls Aloud singer said: 'It's like a comedy – everyone's so flash. It's like, who's got the best watch on, who's got the best bag, which wife is dressed the best, which wife's got the best hair? I'm like, "I've got my own career." It really annoys me when people try to call me a footballer's wife. Footballers' wives have no careers and live off their husbands' money.'

As a couple, Wayne and Coleen have enormous earnings potential. Many of the deals that have flooded Wayne's way – Nike, Coca Cola, a £5 million deal with HarperCollins for a five-book deal – have also come Coleen's way. As previously stated, she now promotes Nike women's wear, and has also been signed up by Harper Collins to write a book giving tips on health and beauty.

But Wayne's red mist temper, which saw him sent off in the game against Portugal at the World Cup – and subsequently saw England's dreams end in tears – is a threat to the couple's earning power. Renowned for his tinderbox temper, Wayne is said to have received anger management counselling but fans and players alike watched in horror as he appeared to stamp on the groin of Portugal defender Ricardo Carvalho.

As Portugal's Cristiano Ronaldo appeared to urge the ref to show the red card, angry Wayne foolishly yelled and pushed him in an ugly ten-man melee. Then Wayne, the striker on whom England's hopes depended with Michael Owen crocked, was manhandled from the field, kicking out in fury, by a member of the team's backroom staff.

Wayne, who had earlier in the tournament delighted fans by recovering quickly from a broken metatarsal, went from hero to zero as the media cast him as an idiot who cost England the best chance of winning the World Cup since 1966.

Coleen wept openly as her man was sent off, aware of the downpour of blame and shame that Wayne's behaviour would invite.

He even vowed that he would never play with Ronaldo again, despite the fact that the two are Manchester United team-mates, creating a major crisis for the club's boss Sir Alex Ferguson.

Wayne insisted that he didn't deliberately stamp on Carvalho and that he was 'disappointed' that Ronaldo had got involved.

He said: 'If you ask any player and indeed any fan, they will tell you that I am straight and honest in the way I play. I bear no ill feeling to Cristiano but I am disappointed that he got involved. I want to say absolutely categorically that I did not put my foot down on Carvalho intentionally. He slid in from behind me and unfortunately ended up in a position where my foot was inevitably going to end up as I kept my balance.'

Just two days later, Coleen was at the launch of Must Have, a clothing range by George for Asda which has earned her a whopping £3 million sponsorship deal. The danger is that if Wayne's sponsorship deals begin to fall, it will have a domino effect on Coleen.

Wayne has already amassed a £10 million fortune – and Coleen £5.5 million. But experts agree that he has the potential to earn at least ten times that.

Says his agent Paul Stretford: 'Provided he stays fit, Wayne has the potential to earn upwards of £100 million over the next decade or so. We're emphasising that, unlike Beckham, we won't be preoccupied with fickle fashion. Wayne is a product of his environment – the streets and the terraces. He is not manufactured, he is a real person and I don't want him to lose that appeal.'

That means Coleen is also currently dependent on Wayne staying fit and retaining the same down-to-earth appeal. Leading PR analyst Mark Borkowski, who has worked with everyone from Mikhail Gorbachev to Diego Maradona and who handles Noel Edmonds, believes Coleen needs to widen her appeal.

He said: 'It's all very well spending half your day in the gym but the problem is that you need to keep doing it. If she's to be presented as some kind of lifestyle guru, she could end up like Victoria Beckham, extremely thin and a poor role model for young women.

Of course, what endears Coleen to people at the moment is that she seems more approachable, more accessible. She is the girl-next-door who made good and other girls feel an affinity with her, they way they don't with Victoria. That difference is most likely because Victoria did have her own career and was more famous than her husband when she was a Spice Girl.

That might serve as a lesson to Coleen who is a likeable girl who works hard at her image. It is admirable that she wants to make her own way, by going to drama school, rather than merely jumping on the gravy train, which will be short-lived.

Mark continues: Coleen is perfect fodder for the likes of *More, Heat, Closer, Cosmopolitan*, the kind of magazines that appeal to young women and she will make a fortune out of modelling for them. She's a down to earth girl, not a starlet or icon, and young women will buy into her style. She could, for example, front a campaign to reinvent a brand like Avon. She is an ambassador for the ordinary woman which gives her fantastic potential for various types of business who want to appeal to the ordinary girl in the street.

'As long as she is with Wayne the couple will make a mint. Unlike Victoria, Coleen is only famous because she is with Wayne. If they break up, she will quickly disappear back into obscurity.'

Wise words. Clearly, if Wayne and Coleen don't get their approach right, it would be very easy for them to fall off the sponsorship radar, especially after what happened at the World Cup. And of course, there are always other media darlings waiting in the wings to take the sponsors' cash. Chief among them at the moment, Theo Walcott and his girlfriend Melanie Slade.

Melanie is a different kettle of fish to Coleen. She is more sophisticated, she photographs well, she is petite and she has media savvy thanks to having a father in PR.

Wayne and Coleen need to be careful not to be engulfed by the cult of greed.

Says Mark: 'Whether you are forgiven a mistake by the public is very often governed by the way you are perceived to have behaved; if you've been high and mighty, you are much less likely to be given a break.'

Of course Wayne is already a patron of a hospital charity in Liverpool and the documentary Coleen presented about the funding of children's hospices did her a world of good, proving she has compassion and the ability to take on a difficult subject and make it sound simple. It has given her substance and shows she is trying to use her fame for the good of others too.

The Outside Organisation's top PR Stuart Bell, whose clients include Westlife, Ronan Keating, Dannii Minogue and Sir Paul McCartney, agrees that Coleen's appeal lies in her sincerity.

Says Stuart: 'Coleen is a positive role model for aspiring young teenagers. She is compassionate, kind and doesn't abuse her position. She's not the kind of girl who would demand to have a whole store closed down just so she could pop in to buy a new dress.'

When she was first introduced to the public, Coleen was subjected to scorn, dubbed as a chav only famous for her shopping skills and who stuck by her man despite his sex life being exposed in the press.

But, says Stuart, 'That was harsh. Any young girl from her background and in her position would have done exactly the same. A majority of other footballer's wives and girlfriends do just as much shopping as Coleen – and discover their partners have been unfaithful – but have never been scorned in the way she was.

'I feel a lot of assumptions were made about Coleen in the early days and partly that may have been her fault because she never co-operated with the media. Nobody could blame her for being nervous of sticking her head above the parapet after the mud she had slung her way. But that has all changed since she did the *Vogue* shoot.'

What you see is what you get with Coleen. She doesn't try to manipulate or suddenly re-invent herself with a dramatic make-over. That is when insincerity sets in and invites cynicism.

'It is laudable that she has used her position to help others and it appears that that is something she enjoys. The [children's hospices] documentary gave substance to Coleen and she could further help her image by increasing her charity profile.

'I believe the public are fond of Coleen. They have watched her grow up in the spotlight and she is still evolving. Of course, she will make some mistakes along the way. Nobody is perfect, but instead of complaining and criticising the media, Coleen seems to learn. I think that shows a gritty determination and proves she is capable of achieving a lot in her own right.'

And she is already turning the tide in her favour. If you open any kids' magazine there is nearly always an article on Coleen – and they never mention

Wayne. She has become a personality in her own right but is not just famous for being famous. She uses her fame for good and refuses to conform – yes, she does beautiful fashion shoots but what she wears is always what she likes, there's no artifice which is often unappealing.

With some high profile sponsors already in the bag, Coleen is taking huge steps in the right direction. But, warns Stuart, she needs to be on her guard. 'I think she needs to be careful that she doesn't spread herself too thin and should concentrate instead on her charity work,' he advises. 'That not only earns her the respect she deserves but it gives her gravitas.

'She is still only a young girl, which is easy to forget. Yet at twenty years old she is adamant that she will forge ahead with her own career and be a person in her own right. So far, she seems to be on track. I think the public have come to admire her for her sincerity, warmth and good-natured kindness.'

Public relations expert Karon Maskill, whose clients include actress Samantha Morton, Eddie Izzard and Helena Bonham Carter, believes Coleen has become an ambassador for the ordinary girl in the street.

She said: 'Coleen has become an inspirational character to many young girls today. In our current celebrity climate she appears to have it all, the footballer boyfriend, the designer clothes, the detached house, complete with dream lifestyle. However, what makes Coleen stand out against the backdrop of immaculately coiffeured, plastic, sporting girlfriends and wives is her almost iconic girl-next-door image.'

Karon continues: 'Coleen has grown up in front of the world's media and many young girls have grown up alongside her. We have seen this shy, innocent teenager turn into an attractive, self-confident young woman. However her home style charm is down to the fact that she is refreshingly unremarkable. Pretty, moderately intelligent but unsophisticated and unexceptional in every way.'

Coleen has lived her teenage years in a goldfish bowl and, rather like Kylie, Charlotte Church and Princess Diana before her, the nation believes they own a small part of her. Pictures in celebrity magazines confirm that she makes frequent fashion faux paux, has cellulite, can put on weight and gets the odd blemish and countless teenagers up and down the country look at her and think, 'She is just like me so if she can have all that, so can I.'

The other endearing quality is the love story between her and Wayne. Everyone is a sucker for a romance and theirs comes straight out of Mills and

Boon. Where once upon a time young girls looked to find a handsome prince and become a Royal, the ultimate dream now is to find a footballer and live the glamorous, decadent lifestyle of the rich and totally pampered – a dream Coleen herself had as a schoolgirl.

And, says Karon, it's a fairytale lifestyle that can continue to flourish. 'Coleen's future is rosy as long as she remains part of Team Rooney,' she says. 'Together they have to potential to be long-term media players. We can expect the showbiz wedding, the Portland babies, the *OK!* shoots. And because Team Rooney are a real-life soap opera the public will lap it up.'

However, the early signs are that Coleen may buck the trend. When details of her and Wayne's private life became the subject of media frenzy, she behaved with great dignity proving there is more to Coleen than meets the eye. She has a steely determination which makes her unhappy to sit at home, lunch, shop and play the footballers' wife indefinitely. And she's already taking steps to carve out her own career.

Concludes Karon: 'She could launch herself as a children's TV presenter, perhaps launch her own fashion line or perfume and, of course, work for her adopted charity. Coleen may hate the Press intrusion into every aspect of her life but the realities are that once tasted, fame and attention are difficult drugs to give up.'

Consumer PR expert Christina Wright, managing director of PR4, believes Coleen has the potential to become as big a celebrity as Victoria Beckham.

She said: 'Our perception of Coleen has transformed dramatically over the last few years. She was the girl who got lucky when her boyfriend became a football hero and celebrated by spending his money on extravagant shopping sprees and hair extensions. She was the girl who seemed to have hit the jackpot and invited envy because of it.

'However, her fiancé's sexual shenanigans, a few fashion mistakes and a documentary later, and our perceptions have changed. We've warmed to Coleen for her honest approach and admire the way she enjoys being the other half of England's biggest football hero.

'Where the typical trophy wives will pose, pout and slim down in a bid for adoration, Coleen remains true to herself whether in Prada or Primark and smiles for the cameras as though she's genuinely content.

'Coleen has skilfully used the media to move from unlikely celebrity to the girl we all like to read about. Her grounded nature coupled with her new found sense of style means she is appealing to a plethora of brands from Asda to Asprey and she is the envy of girls across the country.

'She does have the potential to become a great British celebrity like Victoria Beckham before her, but one recognized for her worth rather than her wardrobe. She has yet to reveal her true talents. Her prospects are dependent on her aptitude for her chosen path and if she's good, she has the potential to become a seriously hot property in her own right.

'Because she is "Mrs Rooney" we will always take an interest in what she wears and her relationship, but equally if she remains Coleen she gives us that much-needed balance against the typical footballers' wives and proves that you really can have it all, keep your ego in check and remain normal.'

PR consultant Phil Hill, whose clients include Heather Mills McCartney and IPC Magazines, also believes Coleen's appeal lies in her accessibility. He thinks Coleen could earn anywhere between £20–£25 million in the next ten years but there is a giant 'but' – she must remain the girlfriend of Wayne Rooney and his career must continue to soar.

'Her fresh, natural personality has great appeal, but is not enough on its own,' he says. 'Readers of newspapers and magazines relate to her because she is one of them, she is not remote, she makes mistakes in the fashion stakes, her hair is sometimes glorious, sometimes awful, but to endure as a fashion icon she needs the Wayne factor.'

Most observers agree that Coleen needs Wayne alongside her to continue to maximise her earning potential and public profile but, with several lucrative endorsements behind her and a possible TV presenting career about to take off, she has made a pretty good start as an independent woman. One nil for Girl Power. The Spice Girls (maybe even Victoria) would be proud.

CHAPTER TEN

my wayne did it the hard way

IF there is one thing that irritates Coleen more than anything, it is suggestions that Wayne has had it easy.

The couple now lead a dream lifestyle, a million miles away from the council estate where they first met as childhood sweethearts. They have a fleet of cars, a home built to their own specifications and the kind of holidays only the super-rich can afford.

It's the kind of life which drives millions of people to buy a lottery ticket every week in the hope that they might win a slice of a better future. But Coleen is fed up with envious people showering Wayne with criticism for his success. She told me: 'Sometimes people act like Wayne has won the lottery or something. But nobody deserves his success more than Wayne. Nothing came easy, that's not the way it was.'

Indeed, that's not the way it was at all. Wayne's life as a teenage footballer involved training five nights a week and a full match every Saturday or Sunday. During the week, he wouldn't get home until 9.30 p.m., too late to play with his friends. His pals would be going to the cinema or hanging out in the street together while Wayne was putting his kit on to train.

'There were times I didn't want to go, I just wanted to give it all up' he told me. 'I wanted to hang with my mates, go to the cinema, just do normal stuff. My mum and dad would say to me, "If you want to be a professional footballer, you have to make sacrifices".'

Then they would put Wayne in the car and drive him to the training ground. He would go to school and then training – that was his life.

'I knew if I didn't do it, I wouldn't become a professional footballer, but it was still hard,' he says. 'I was only a kid and I felt I was missing out on life because I couldn't be with the other lads, couldn't do the things they were doing.

'I loved my football, really loved it, but at a young age what you most want to do is be one of the gang, hang out with your mates and just kick a ball around in the street. But I had to be disciplined to get where

I've got now and I've worked hard for it. I do not see myself as a hero, whatever people say or write about me.

'I've still got a long way to go and, if you believe all the things said about you when you're doing well, you have to look at them when you're not having the same success. You only need one bad game and things change and that can knock your confidence if you let it.'

There was one person who always remained at his side and shared his moments of despondency – Coleen, an ambitious girl herself, understood only too well the pressures Rooncy felt.

She told me: 'I always encouraged Wayne, I never asked him to put me before his football. I wouldn't have expected that – and he never expected that of me. He knew I wanted to be an actress and was into my studies and accepted that meant I had to revise.

'We both accepted that the other had commitments, but we always spent as much time together as we could. He'd usually come round to my house. He was my first boyfriend. Up until I met Wayne I wasn't that into boys, I was into working hard to achieve my ambitions.

'I was a bit nervous when I first started seeing Wayne but the more I got to know him the more I felt comfortable. We were similar people – our ambition made us compatible. We understood each other without ever having to spell it out or explain.'

Wayne's every waking moment was occupied by football and he spent most of his time in the classroom day-dreaming about his heroes rather than concentrating on his work.

He admits, 'I look back now and realise I should have given more time to my schoolwork but, when you're a kid, you don't listen to the best advice. Mainly, it was football that got me into trouble. I wasn't interested in anything else and just wanted to play all the time.'

He would often go to school looking smart – black blazer, trousers, tie and white shirt. But, by the time he got home, he would often had rips in his trousers, caused by sliding tackles and heroic goal line clearances. 'Mum would be upset and give me a clip because it means she had to buy me a new pair,' says Wayne. 'She'd never let me go to school with ripped trousers. No way!'

Wayne's obsession with football earned him a few detentions, too, as he spent a lot of time running out of school to the chip shop or to have a kick about. When his mum and dad got to hear about it he was usually grounded. And that caused a problem for his love life – it meant he could only text Coleen.

For Wayne, school was mainly an opportunity for football practice and not academic study. 'The only subject I liked at school was maths,' he explains. 'It's the only GCSE I sat. By then, I was sixteen and already knew I had a future at Everton so I couldn't see the point of doing more.'

By contrast, Coleen passed eleven GCSE exams and was about to begin A-levels when Wayne's star suddenly burst into the public consciousness. That stunning goal in the game against Arsenal, which left England keeper David Seaman sitting on his butt, meant the touchpaper to fame had been lit for Wayne. And for Coleen, it meant putting up with bitching by the other girls at school – and having the paparazzi on her tail. She had little choice but to give up her studies, after anguished discussions with her parents when Wayne promised to look after her.

He said: 'Just a few years ago, I could still go out in the streets and play footie with my mates but now I can't, and it is the same for Coleen because she is with me. When we go out, I am constantly asked for autographs, which I don't mind, but it makes having a conversation difficult!

'The thing is, my circumstances have changed but I haven't, and Coleen is one of the few people who understand that. She knows me better than anyone else, she is the one who is around at night when we are on my own and I'm feeling dead bad because my foot is in plaster, or because I haven't played as well as I wanted to.

'She stays strong for me and gives me strength. I get strength from her, she is always positive and, anyway, I know she loves me, the real me, not the Wayne Rooney everybody chants for on the pitch. To Coleen, I am still the boy who kicked a ball around in the street. That's not going to change and nor am I.'

Coleen admits that she loves the opportunity to dress up in her finery and dine at expensive restaurants or hotels but she told me: 'That's not us. That's just a bonus. We prefer our own lifestyle – seeing our mates and just being normal at home. We treasure that.'

Even as a boy, Rooney's only goal was to be a footballer. Instinct urged him on, the magic in his feet casting its spell as the engrossed six-year-old aimed shot after shot at the makeshift goal in his backyard, dreaming of his hero Alan Shearer and hoping one day, just perhaps, that he might aim for a real goal, playing for his beloved Everton or even, by a stretch of the imagination, for England.

The boy had a dream and had already etched his

future into the paintwork of his bedroom window overlooking a jaded suburban street in Liverpool – 'Rooney, W…EFC', it read. But as he carefully scratched his yearning into the splintered wooden surround, the little boy could never have imagined how quickly his dream would come true.

Today, Wayne Rooney is a megastar, a Manchester United and England hero and, to some, including pop star Robbie Williams, 'simply a god.' He may be just twenty years old but he's been called a genius, likened to the legendary footballer Pelé – by the man himself – and described by England's former goal-getter Gary Lineker as 'potentially the best England player of my lifetime.' For good measure, Lineker adds, 'It beggars belief a kid could be as good as him.'

Wayne understands exactly how he feels because he is still pinching himself too.

He says: 'Just a few years ago I couldn't have dreamed all this. When I look back, I can hardly believe it. It sometimes feels a bit mad to be regarded as England's centre forward at my age. It's the sort of thing you pretend to be when you're knocking a ball about in the street.'

Old habits die hard and Wayne has already attracted mutterings from neighbours by belting a ball noisily and repeatedly against a wall, just like he did at Gran Mavis'.

Gran Mavis was a rock for Wayne's parents in turbulent times. His dad, Wayne Snr, was a hod-carrier, jobbing as a casual labourer on building sites. Work was scarce and frequent spells of unemployment left a legacy of determination that the same fate would not befall his sons. Mum Jeanette worked at two jobs to make ends meet, by day as a dinner lady at the all-boys De La Salle Roman Catholic High School where Wayne would later become a pupil, and by night as a cleaner at the all-girls school where Coleen was already a student.

Wayne and his two brothers Graham and John often stayed with their grandma while their parents struggled to make ends meet. A doughty, no nonsense woman, gran Mavis helped keep the lads on the straight and narrow, dishing out a clip round the ear when they strayed out of line and soothing words, accompanied by an Everton mint, when the world seemed glaringly unjust.

Wayne was an unassuming boy, quiet and shy. But, even back then, he smouldered with a steadily burning desire, one which urged him out of bed into the crisp morning light to conjure up the magic in his feet – often to the disappoval of his gran.

While others slept, the determined lad would sneak outside at 7 a.m., often alone except for his scuffed football, and zealously practise his shots, waking the neighbours and leaving his exasperated gran to tear after him before another area of paint and render was blasted off her wall.

'Nan didn't think it was funny,' remembers Wayne. 'She'd hear the pebbles fall from the wall and yell, "WAAAYNE!" and I'd get a clip round the ear but I'd still be there first thing in the morning, just kicking the ball over and over.

'I remember the first time I kicked a ball around the garden at five years old – I've wanted to play ever since. The feeling of scoring a goal, even when you were a little boy, was amazing. Once I started scoring, I didn't want to stop. I remember me and my cousins used to put our coats down as goalposts and pretend to be our heroes – I was always Gazza, Alan Shearer or Duncan Ferguson.

'And I remember scoring my first goal in the playground, it was amazing, everybody ran over and congratulated me. It was such an amazing feeling – I still get that now.'

Yet as a schoolboy Wayne wasn't solely concerned with football. His other love was *Teenage Mutant Ninja Turtles*. 'I was mad about the Turtles, we all were at school' he recalls. 'We used to wrap our ties around our heads and pretend to be ninjas, throwing each other down on to the floor and doing all the ninja moves – I was always Rafael, he was my favourite.

'I also had a mountain bike as a kid and rollerblades – mine were navy blue and we used to think we looked really cool with those on tracking around the streets – I was actually quite good.'

Wayne had just made the Everton youth team, in 2001 when his gran Mavis died, a devastating blow which left him reeling. He said: 'She died from lung cancer. I had begged her to give up smoking – the same as I have with my mum – but she never did. While nan was ill, I used to stay over. I'd go and get her shopping from Kwiksave, walking there and taking a taxi back, and help round the house with cleaning and the like.

'When she died I was devastated – obviously I loved her. At her funeral I wrote a speech and read it out to everyone. I'd never spoken in public before, it was hard, but I wanted to do it for my nan.

'My one regret is that nan never got to see my play for England but I think she'd be proud of me. I still think about her every day and visit her grave, to lay flowers. She was like my rock.'

These days, it is Coleen who is Wayne's rock, an immovable fixture in his life, through good and bad times, through allegations and revelations that would destroy others. Some ignorantly reckon

Coleen hangs on to Wayne, after devastating allegations that he slept with a hooker, because she's in too deep – giving up the lifestyle that she now has with Wayne would be a near impossibility when she has nothing else to offer.

But those who underestimate Coleen do so at their peril. She may seem soft as a pussycat but she guards Wayne with all the pride of a lion – and she is a bright girl who could, if she wished, return to her studies and enter University.

She remains with Wayne because she was counselled by her parents to do so, but also because she loves him. Her parents, who have been wed for more than twenty five years, know a relationship means compromise, understanding and forgiveness. As they told their distraught daughter, 'Nobody is perfect.'

Their strong Catholic belief would have meant confession for Wayne, not only to them, but to Coleen. Nobody should imagine that would have been easy – nor that Wayne failed in the task. He loves Coleen and he returns to her because she makes him feel safe, the only woman he can trust to understand him and be with him for who he is, not what he has earned.

Other girls from his past have suddenly popped up, trying to gain his interest – girls who had no interest in him when he was a mere lad from the run down Croxteth council estate.

Says Wayne: 'Girls do throw themselves at me now but both me and Coleen know why. It leaves no impression on me at all and Coleen knows she is the only one for me. I want her to be my wife. I can't say more than that.'

Wayne is now the biggest star since George Best, even eclipsing David Beckham. Coleen has a lot to live up to and she needs to fill her own time with her own success to feel good and happy about herself. Living in the light of his reflected glory while having nothing to say for herself could only be disastrous.

That is not to say that she doesn't give 100 per cent to her boyfriend, nursing him through his injuries and protecting him from chancers. What it means is that he is free to focus on his football without worrying whether she is occupied or unhappy.

Coleen's newfound confidence and career as a style and sex symbol may be short-lived but she is enjoying herself as never before. To dedicate all her time to a man who is often absent would be a waste – it would lead to too much pressure on him, when there is already so much expectation and also too much pressure on her to measure up, compete or merely be exhausted by his emotional demands.

The couple seem to have worked out a balance which is still experimental but appears to work. They may still be young but they are wisely counselled and have been taught the value of keeping a relationship alive by being autonomous. If anything, Wayne is more reliant on Coleen for salving his ego and telling him the truth when others merely pander.

Coleen told me: 'I don't have to tiptoe round Wayne. We know each other too well and he knows he will always get the truth from me and vice versa. People can say what they like about us, but only we know how it is. That's how our relationship is and that is why we trust each other. I don't care what anybody else thinks. All that matters is what we think.'

When Rooney made his competitive debut for England, thrown into the cauldron of a European Championship tie against Turkey at Sunderland's Stadium of Light, in April 2003, there were three fans he wanted to please more than any others – his mum, dad and Coleen.

Like Coleen, Wayne is close to his two brothers Graham and John and just as protective and supportive of them as his parents were of him. He's given both a nest-egg, and treated them to the best that money can buy in everything from sporting equipment to Playstations to CD and DVD players – the kind of things he could only dream of having as a boy himself.

Given the meagre income Jeanette and Wayne Snr managed to pull in each week, it meant the family lived on a tight budget, working together to make the best use of their money. Like others on the estate in Croxteth, the boys often wore hand-me-down clothes; Jeanette's weekly treat was a game of bingo, and Wayne Snr's was a pint or two down his local pub The Wezzy or a trip to nearby Aintree racecourse, where he sometimes took his excited lads to watch the horses thundering home.

The couple kept laying hens in their garden for fresh eggs, and there was also Wayne Snr's pigeon loft, his prized birds having been trained to return home in races against competitors, sometimes being released on day trips to the nearby Welsh mountains.

The boys were encouraged to take part in sport, as a way of keeping them off the streets and to instil in them discipline, and in the silent hope that they might excel.

Wayne's mum had a reputation as a no-nonsense woman, one who would brook no argument from the teenagers who lined up in the dinner queue while she was on duty at De La Salle School.

Wayne's former agent Peter McIntosh remembers:

'In the day, Jeanette would work as a dinner lady and then go and do another job. I remember she did so many hours she often didn't have the time to go and watch Wayne play for Everton. She was the breadwinner because Wayne's dad was out of work. She knew that everything relied on her. Wayne never wanted for anything, whether it was training shoes or money for going out. Both of Wayne's parents went without so they could do the best for their sons.'

Jeanette ruled her sons with a rod of iron, determined to keep them on the straight and narrow but always there as the first line of defence if anybody dared criticise her boys. As Wayne said: 'I'm more scared of my mum than I am of Sven-Goran Eriksson! She's always ready to hand me a slap if I get out of line.'

But she was also ready to hand out a piece of her mind if she felt her lads were being treated unfairly. She took a dim view when her youngest son John was ditched from the Everton Academy for being too fat, marching down to the training ground and remonstrating with the coaches. Fuming Jeanette insisted John had the potential to be every bit as good as Wayne and, within days, John was reinstated, testament to Jeanette's forceful belief in justice.

Said Peter McIntosh: 'Jeanette just knows what is

best for her lads and believes in them. She is what you might call a strong character. She isn't one of these women who doesn't know anything about football. She knows the offside rule, she knew when a player was playing well or badly. She never criticised Wayne. She was always upbeat and she told him he was doing well.

'She was a very strong woman, a lot like Wayne in many ways. She was a quiet, independent type who just got on with her life and her sons were at the centre of it.'

Jeanette's reputation as a tough cookie even travelled as far as the England squad. When once asked before a match what time kick-off was, Liverpool's Steven Gerrard quipped, 'When Wayne's mum gets here!"

Like most riled woman, Jeanette had the capacity to make grown men quake in their boots when it came to her brood, but she's a softie at heart. She wept when Wayne scored his first Premiership goal; she wept when he first pulled on a Three Lions shirt and she wept when he scored his first goal for England.

And so did his overwhelmed dad. He was pictured wiping a tear from his eye as Wayne blew the socks off everyone at Euro 2004, even jubilantly punching the air and performing a spontaneous little jig in front of the delirious crowds chanting his son's name.

Says Jeanette: 'Wayne's just like his dad, they're like two peas in a pod. We're all really excited about seeing all the games Wayne plays in, no matter where. I've always been proud of him – even as a lad, he played for a team called Pye FC and he won his first Golden Boot with them after scoring the most goals in the BT Challenge Cup competition. I've still got that trophy. I'm the proudest mum in the world.'

Wayne's family are the first to recognise that he hasn't had his head turned by fame. His aunt Janet Gildea, his mum's sister, says: 'We all just treat him as good old Wayne at family get-togethers – he gets no superstar treatment and he doesn't want any. He comes to visit at least once a week and just sits down and chats with a can of Coke like the rest of the kids.'

Her daughter, Wayne's cousin Toni, often watched matches with the star long before his name became a touchstone. She says: 'We used to watch the matches with Wayne's dad at first but, as we got older and wanted more independence, we started going on our own, getting the bus into town and getting chips before kick-off.

'Wayne was aged about fourteen at the time, but he was already a famous face at Goodison Park. He had signed on the books for the Everton Youth Academy, was playing regularly and scoring goals. So all the fans on the terraces knew who he was and there was already talk that he was going to be something special.

'People used to tease him about me, asking whether I was his sweetheart. Most fans would want to chat to Wayne and start asking us questions about where we went on dates, but he just got dead embarrassed by it. Wayne wasn't interested in any girl but Coleen back then, all he would talk about was football.

'I was a bit of a tomboy back then, so I got on with male cousins the best. I used to tease Wayne a little that girls would never be interested him if he spent all his time playing football but look at him now!

'But Wayne still comes round to our house. There's nothing more he likes than to have a chat about things happening in our lives. He's interested in the family, normal things, but he likes to treat us too. He bought season tickets for my uncle, granddad, my cousin and me in the main stand. Wayne has always been close to his family and wants to share his success.'

His nan Patricia, who also lives on the Croxteth estate, is proud as punch of her grandson, one of 37 grandchildren. She's recently been provided with a pacemaker and is under strict instructions not to jump or punch the air when her grandson scores. But it doesn't stop Patricia and her husband William sharing the joy of Wayne's success.

She told *The Sun*: 'We're all so proud of him. I'm the proudest gran in England and my husband Billy feels the same way. We've decorated our house with pictures of Wayne, we even have one in the window, and everyone around Croxteth knows who I am.

'I get so excited when I watch him play, I can't look at the telly. So I watch the match in bed and, when he's going for goal, I put my hand over my eyes. I remember when he did his cartwheel at Euro 2004, it was spectacular. We're all hoping we'll see another one at the World Cup.'

Her husband Billy added: 'I'd die happy after seeing that. It makes me cry when I think about him and I go to bed with tears on my pillow. He's dead quiet and shy but he's got the heart of a lion.'

Sadly for Wayne the World Cup goals didn't come but, to paraphrase his granddad, Wayne has the heart of the Three Lions – and with Coleen at his side he's all set to roar.

CHAPTER ELEVEN

the new aroostocracy

COLEEN McLoughlin is set to become the 'First Lady' of an exclusive new set of footballing aristocrats who will rewrite society's rules on wealth and inheritance.

Previously, the wealthy were categorised as having acquired their riches through either 'old' money or 'new' money.

Now the advent of the rich and youthful footballers who are paid millions of pounds each year has led the monied classes to define a new level of wealth which they have dubbed the Football – or FB – Index. (Obviously a play on the more traditional FT Index used by the Stock Exchange).

It is the most significant indication yet of how the

millions of pounds being earned each year by very young men with very rare skills is rebalancing the whole of our society. And that fact that their wives and girlfriends like to shop until they drop is even helpful to the economy.

Coleen, for example, is the youngest self-made woman ever to appear in *The Sunday Times* Rich List – she has swelled her coffers to £5.5 million with sponsorship deals and photo shoots, as we have seen. Yet just three years ago she was a nobody, an average girl in clumpy black shoes and puffa jacket queueing for chips on a desolate council estate in Liverpool.

Now, she is beyond middle class – an 'aroostacrat' thanks to her fiancé's £50,000-a-week salary and the kind of spending habit which would see the Sultan of Brunei bat an eyelid.

Footballers and their families, those in the FB Index, have rewritten all the rules that apply to both old and new money in the way they accumulate their riches. In less than one lifetime, tremendous wealth is being created that will form dynasties that could go on for generations.

What is so significant about this phenomenon is the rapidity with which fortunes are being accumulated. There are more than a dozen players in the Premiership who are still in their teens and who can describe themselves as multi-millionaires. And there are just as many on the Continent.

It is all about the laws of supply and demand. When a skill as rare as that of Wayne Rooney is discovered there is the equivalent of a Klondike gold rush to invest in the product – the footballer himself. Consequently, through shrewd management, which Wayne has in abundance, there is an immediate delivery of millions of pounds.

The investors – football clubs who sign the players and up to six or eight commercial giants like Coke – are happy to agree to long-term contracts, often paid up front to ward off predators. It means that a young footballer barely out of his apprenticeship can move in to a £2 million mansion and drive a £150,000 car without even blinking.

In the 2006 *Sunday Times* Rich List, the bible of the wealthy, Coleen is listed jointly with Wayne as being worth £20 million. Broken down, the assessment is that she has a personal fortune of £5.5 million from modelling, endorsements and publishing. But that in itself does not tell the full story. In the previous year's list the couple's worth was put at £6 million. That means that it has increased by more than 300 per cent in twelve months alone.

At that continuing rate of accumulation it is easy

to see why Professor Tom Cannon of the University of Kingston wrote that the young footballer will be the first in history to become a billionaire.

Of course, the duo are not the only rich sporting couple. But they are the youngest and the ones with the greatest wealth-making potential to join the exclusive FB index. And their emergence is already triggering a social metamorphosis that has never been seen before. It immediately catapults people from one strata of society to another.

The working class boy without the benefit of a great education will be the last of his line to live in council housing and go to a state school. Tremendous amounts of wealth will be shifted into the control of those who would previously have been described as working class or in some cases deprived.

But they will not be regarded in society as the lucky neighbours next door who won the lottery. That can happen to anybody at random, even if it only happens to a few. The football aristocrats will amass not only great wealth but also respect for doing it by using their talent.

The perfect example of what could happen to Coleen and Wayne is already in evidence in the form of the Beckhams. In the same Rich List, they are placed as a couple as the 67th richest people in Britain with a fortune of just under £90 million.

This is astonishing for a boy brought up in a sparse household in east London and a girl who came from a solid middle-class background in the Home Counties. But nobody can deny that they have earned their wealth, even if some would say it is disproportionate to the contribution they have made to society.

Beckham is easily the most famous footballer in the world with a tremendous sense of self promotion which he has used time and time again to broker fabulous promotional deals. And Victoria, aka Posh Spice, was a singer in the most successful British girl group of all time, who over a space of five years conquered the pop charts around the world, accumulating a fortune as she went.

The 'disproportionate' argument fails on the grounds that whatever they have, they have earned by utilising rare skills. That cannot be said of a member of the old aristocracy who simply inherited their forefathers' wealth.

The Beckhams live an opulent life style. They have a large estate in Sawbridgeworth in Hertfordshire and a £4 million mansion in Spain where England superstar David plays for Real Madrid. Their life has no restrictions, bolstered by their £90 million fortune. It is not just that they have become wealthy themselves, but that they are, by definition, redistributing huge amounts of money.

Michael Owen, an England team-mate of Rooney and Beckham, is a perfect example of how his amassed riches are redistributed in a way that has never been seen before. He was brought up on Deeside just over the border into north Wales. His father was a moderately successful footballer. Owen was one of the youngest ever English international footballers and goal-scorers.

He lives on a very large country estate and in his early twenties he had moved half a dozen members of his family into new homes that were all in the same street and owned by him. Having moved to Newcastle United, he regularly commutes to work by helicopter and he invests heavily in blood-stock to feed his love of horse racing.

All these factors contribute to what the Americans call 'trickle down' economics. If you have a big estate you have to decorate it, build swimming pools and employ people to wash your cars. You need housekeepers, gardeners and mechanics to look after your fleet of cars. Coleen needs hairdressers, couturiers, make-up people, stylists and a personal assistant.

All this financial activity stimulates the economy.

Every time Wayne buys a new car he is keeping a salesman in work. When the couple go out to dinner a lucky waiter not only has a job for the night but usually a hefty tip.

But the FB's are not just stimulating the economy, they are U-turning their own family histories. Very few footballers ever went to anything other than a state school.

One exception is the Chelsea star Frank Lampard who is the only soccer star in the world who has an A grade in Latin at O level. His father Frank Lampard Snr clearly thought it was worth investing some of the money he made as a footballer – modest by today's standards – in his children's education.

That will happen more and more. The children of footballers will go to top schools like Wellington College, Millfield, Charterhouse and even Eton.

There have been few examples of truly great footballers spawning equally talented sons. Instead of crossing their fingers and hoping that their children will display some naturally great talent, footballers are more likely to invest in a great education. Their advisors will tell them that it is a great long-term investment and iconic footballing individuals like Gary Lineker, who has four sons, have already gone down this route.

Whilst FBs as famous as Coleen and Wayne will

always be derided by both old and new money types because of the perceived chav factor, that will not be the case for their children. In one generation FBs can move from very basic working class to educated and informed aristocracy. And because of the scale of wealth they will generate, it will be a permanent move.

Unlike a Pools or Lottery winner there is no chance of their vastly improved status in life ever disappearing. Firstly they will make too much money during the course of their fifteen-year careers to lose again in a few years afterwards. And secondly, all their money will be managed and invested by highly paid, highly competent financiers.

But the money is now taken for granted.

The real power that the FBs have in life is a reverse role about who wields power in our modern society.

As recently as twenty years ago footballers and their wives were regarded as the sort of people you had to tolerate at the chairman's Christmas party. The club boss liked to parade his star player who he paid about £3,000 a week. He would then explain to his other guests that footballers are thick and that nobody should expect too much of them.

It doesn't work like that anymore. The biggest and most glamorous party of recent times was thrown by David and Victoria Beckham three weeks before the start of the 2006 World Cup. It was a pre-tournament bash by England's captain to highlight and strengthen England's assault on the enormous challenge ahead.

The guest list would have filled up the A-Z celebrity bible. Royalty was represented by the Duchess of York and her daughter Beatrice. High society restaurateurs? Gordon Ramsay, who created the menu. And celebrity? The Sharon, Ozzy and Kelly Osbourne family.

Now, that's rich.

In years past, before the advent of FBs, you would not have seen a politician from any part of the spectrum trying to get involved in this glitzy and glamorous affair. But today it is vital for any aspiring Parliamentary power broker to get him or herself involved.

In the early years of New Labour, Tony Blair invited the hot people of the day to a party at Number 10 Downing Street. Noel Gallagher of the group Oasis, when offered a glass of champagne responded, 'No way, Where's the lager Tone?'

It was the age of celebrity which was endorsed by the world-wide best selling news magazine *Time* as 'Cool Britannia.' But the age of the influential rock star, stretching back over forty years to the days when John Lennon was calling for peace, has gone.

Today it's the footballer. The FBs announced how influential they are at the Beckham party. There were no politicians on the guest list. Why should there be? If a footballer says Product A is good he has far more influence over the electorate, locally, nationally and worldwide than anybody who has battled his way into the House of Commons to represent 500,000 people.

Footballers are much more powerful now than anybody who seeks power through Parliament. And that was recognised by David Cameron, the leader of the Conservative Party. He was not invited to the Beckham party – but being a savvy new power broker he decided to go anyway.

What an amazing sea change in society. A man who harbours aspirations to become the Prime Minister of a country that used to control one third of the globe, recognised that going to the Beckham party would be good PR for him.

The only problem was that he didn't have an invitation. So he managed to fix himself up with a invitation through the editor of a tabloid newspaper. Though it was billed as a glamorous black-tie affair, Cameron turned up in an open-necked shirt. Nobody's sure why he did that because he comes from 'old money' aristocracy and would have been expected to respect the dress code.

But it meant that as a result he was pictured in every paper.

It is not the first time a politician has sought popularity through sporting achievement to boost their own fame. As Wayne Rooney's career grows and he reaps the awards that his talent is sure to bring, he and Coleen are sure to be courted by politicians.

After Tony Blair's Cool Britannia party, the politicians turned their attention to footballers. The problem was that they wanted to be associated with soccer success at a national level and the England team had been lacking in that since 1966. But they had decided that attaching themselves to our great national team was a vote-winner.

Out of the blue they decided to knight Geoff Hurst, the World Cup hat trick hero from the '66 final. Geoff was secretly taken down to Wembley Stadium, the scene of his greatest glory and the pictures and stories were prepared for his unveiling as our latest soccer knight. Nobody really objected to Hurst receiving the honour. In fact most said that it was way overdue. There had been a long standing feeling that the 'Boys of '66' had not been properly recognised as heroes.

The victorious manager, Alf Ramsey, had become Sir Alf soon after the victory but nevertheless it was felt that, after he was sacked by The Football

Association following the failed 1974 campaign, he became a forgotten man.

Bobby Charlton, a member of the '66 side was knighted after he retired in the mid 70s but of the rest of the boys were forgotten for many years until public demand insisted they be given awards, although none of the others got a knighthood.

For instance, Bobby Moore, the England captain, once labelled by Pelé as the greatest defender in the world, and a team-mate of Hurst's at West Ham, died of cancer in the early 1990s without being knighted.

A year after Geoff Hurst received his knighthood Manchester United won the European Cup. On a glorious night in Barcelona they beat Bayern Munich in a last gasp effort to seal a remarkable season in which they added the domestic double of Premier League and FA Cup to their European crown.

Even before the teams had left the stadium, and in fact as the players were still celebrating out on the pitch, moves were underway to knight the United manager, Scotsman Alex Ferguson.

Alastair Campbell was the head of government information services. Many regarded him as the real deputy Prime Minister because he was so close to PM Tony Blair. Campbell, himself an avid football fan, had become a friend of Ferguson's during an era when Manchester United were sweeping all before them.

In the Nou Camp on the night of United's victory, Campbell was reportedly battling to get to the pitch to confirm that Alex would accept the award. He got as near as a perimeter fence and managed to communicate with the United box who affirmed he would like to become a knight. A few days later the announcement was made.

Since then others like Bobby Robson, a former England manager, have joined the ranks of footballing knights.

But there has never been a young footballing knight. Once upon a time the lifestyle of a young soccer player, even one as squeaky clean as that of David Beckham, would have been considered too flamboyant to qualify for honours bestowed by the Queen. But that is no longer the case. Past lifestyle or even indiscretions don't count any more as is evidenced by the experience of rock stars.

Sir Mick Jagger, Sir Elton John and Sir Paul McCartney have all lived as mega rock stars tainted with experiences with drugs or alcohol. But that didn't stop them being elevated to the highest levels of the establishment.

Whether such recognition will ever come the way of today's soccer young bloods, we will have to wait and see.

So, in terms of society's rich and powerful people,

the modern-day footballer is already there. Top of the list of richest footballing couples is, as described above, the Beckhams.

After that Michael Owen's fortune is rated at £32 million and he comes 10th equal in the list of Britain's richest young people. The Newcastle forward's wealth derives from sponsorship which is boosted by his clean cut image. After that Rio Ferdinand of Manchester United is at 20th place with £22 million. Below him by one place is Frenchman Thierry Henry of Arsenal with £21 million.

Then come Wayne and Coleen at 22nd place with £20 million. His Manchester United team-mate Ruud van Nistelrooy is 31st in the Rich List with a fortune of £18 million.

In joint 35th place are Emile Heskey of Birmingham City and Frank Lampard of Chelsea, who have an estimated £12 million fortune each.

Steven Gerrard is 40th equal. The Liverpool European Cup-winning captain is worth £10million, as is his Australian team-mate Harry Kewell. Freddie Ljungberg of Arsenal has a similar level of wealth.

Chelsea captain John Terry is worth £9 million, Kieron Dyer of Newcastle and Mark Viduka of Middlesbrough are both worth £8 million.

Ashley Cole of Arsenal and Joe Cole of Chelsea have £7 million in the bank each and a whole group of soccer stars have at least £6 million each. They are Juan Pablo Angel of Aston Villa; Craig Bellamy of Blackburn, Michael Essien and Eidur Gudjohnsen of Chelsea, Robbie Keane of Tottenham Hotspur and Phil Neville of Everton.

They all form the new 'aroostocracy', knocking most of the established aristocracy into a cocked hat – and even the royals cannot claim to be squeaky clean when it comes to affairs of the heart.

All this means Coleen has the potential to become a powerful force in her own right. Now Beckham has resigned as England captain and Posh's star has waned, Coleen is in prime position to become football's new First Lady. She has already proved that there is more to her than becoming a mere fashion icon, and that she can handle the strain of being in the limelight without losing her cool or her dignity.

In the last two years Coleen has grown from an ordinary girl hanging out on street corners in downtrodden Croxteth into a woman who refuses to be browbeaten into becoming a typical footballer's girlfriend.

Her sponsorship deals have been carefully chosen to reflect her down-to-earth appeal and her presentation on the plight of hospices for *Tonight with Trevor McDonald* proves she is bright and more than capable of handling a high-brow subject in a way that gave it mass appeal. The fact that Coleen was the presenter was no doubt influential in the government's sudden pledge to donate £27 million towards the funding of hospices.

Coleen is still evolving. She is just twenty years old but has already undergone a dramatic transformation. She is a shrewd woman with a sharp mind behind her shy exterior. She may never be a supermodel but as a role model she has class in spades.